Peanut Butter and Jelly Management

Peanut Butter and Jelly Management

Tales from Parenthood

Lessons for Managers

Chris and Reina Komisarjevsky

Illustrations by Andrea Geller

AMACOM
American Management Association
New York • Atlanta • Brussels • Chicago • Mexico City
San Francisco • Shanghai • Tokyo • Toronto • Washington, D.C.

Special discounts on bulk quantities of AMACOM books are available to corporations, professional associations, and other organizations. For details, contact Special Sales Department, AMACOM, a division of
American Management Association,
1601 Broadway, New York, NY 10019.
Tel.: 212-903-8316   Fax: 212-903-8083
Web site: www.amacombooks.org

This publication is designed to provide accurate and authoritative information in regard to the subject matter covered. It is sold with the understanding that the publisher is not engaged in rendering legal, accounting, or other professional service. If legal advice or other expert assistance is required, the services of a competent professional person should be sought.

Library of Congress Cataloging-in-Publication Data

Komisarjevsky, Chris.
    Peanut butter and jelly management : tales from parenthood lessons for managers / Chris and Reina Komisarjevsky.
        p. cm.
Includes index.
ISBN 0-8144-7062-9 (hardcover)
ISBN 0-8144-7224-9 (paperback)
1. Personnel management. 2. Employee motivation. I. Komisarjevsky, Reina. II. Title.

HF5549.K647 2004
658.3'14—dc21   2003008054

Printing number

10 9 8 7 6 5 4 3 2 1

To all of our children —

Stephen, Matthew, Nicholas, James, Angelica, Michael,

Ted, Katrina, Vera,

. . . and especially to Christopher Michael

who watches over all of them from heaven

Contents

Preface to the Paperback Edition

The more things change ...
The more they stay the same

It's been three years since the publication of *Peanut Butter and Jelly Management*. Times change. The clock moves forward. The world turns. Change is everywhere. At home, the children are getting older (now they are between the ages of nine and fifteen), and all of us are tackling new challenges. At work, nothing stands still. And, in the early years of this new century, the environment for business everywhere could hardly be more demanding.

Yet, when we look back at what we've learned from all of our children by listening, watching, and thinking, these *tales from parenthood, lessons for managers* still seem to be right.

On the surface, we somehow think we should be surprised to find that the lessons are still worth listening to, especially given the drama around the world these days—political tensions, turmoil in the financial markets, and disappointment in the behavior of some business leaders and managers from whom we all had the right to expect much more.

But, in reality, we shouldn't be surprised because the underlying lessons from parenthood are as valid today as yesterday. And it's not all that complicated. It's actually quite simple when you take the time to look beneath the surface and try to focus on the underlying values that motivate, encourage, and help people to live up to their potential.

The key, though, is to look.

To take a different twist on history: On March 30, 1853, Vincent van Gogh was born in the Netherlands, the second of six children. According to almost every biography, he was troubled his entire life. Many considered him insane. In his thirties, still struggling to find himself, he moved to Paris to live with his brother in Montmartre, the famous artist quarter. Painting—portraiture, to be more accurate—was his passion but, with no money to hire artists' models, he decided to invest in a simple mirror.

That mirror was a changing point. It enabled him to

see, to really "look." With it, he was able to look closely at himself and paint what he saw. Over the next years, he painted more than twenty self-portraits, moving through colors from somber browns and grays to bright yellows, reds, greens, and blues as he learned more and more about what he saw. This period of his life culminated in one of his most famous paintings, "Self-Portrait as an Artist," and it is a dramatic illustration of what he saw and how he drew his own reflection.

Few can come close—or might even want to come close—to the genius that was van Gogh. But, regardless, all of us should be eager to seek out our own unique way to see, to really look. If we do, we will see those often very simple lessons of life that truly have an impact on our abilities and on others.

Peanut Butter and Jelly Management was and is a simple technique for doing just that. And, despite all the changes in the world, it appears that the lessons apply today, ever as much as they did yesterday.

Some would argue that difficult times call for greater toughness. There is no question that decision-making must be faster—there is less room and no time for error when the competition is fierce and the availability of resources much less. Of course, there are many times when being tough is important, both in families and in business. But motivating people, encouraging self-esteem, giving others the courage to deal with adversity, fostering teamwork, living strong values, and ensuring open communication—all still are at the forefront of strong leadership, whether the times are good or not.

With this edition, we've added a new chapter, one that is especially relevant for our family and for the stressful times in which business operates today. Titled "When Things Get Tough," it tells the story of our son James being diagnosed with juvenile diabetes and draws a parallel to tackling the unexpected downturns of business in a troubled economy.

And there was a chapter that we didn't write. We wanted very much to talk more about values, especially in light of how important they are to the underpinnings of both families and business. Integrity, doing what is right, is essential. But it often comes at a cost. In business, it might be financial. At home, it might simply be embarrassment.

It is strong values, though, most often passed down from generation to generation or from leader to employee, that *stand the test of time.* This is where the personal example set by the leader, by actions not by words, becomes one of the most powerful elements of leadership.

But we didn't write that chapter, because, on the one hand, we all still have a lot to learn. Both parenting and leadership in business are *works in progress.* They take hard work and determination. None of us is there yet. Certainly we don't have all the answers.

And, on the other hand, we believe that virtually everyone instinctively really does know the difference between what is right and what is wrong. They just need to *listen to what their gut tells them.* It really is that simple.

When *Peanut Butter and Jelly Management* was first published, the respected business newspaper *Financial Times* surprised all of us by writing a book review in which it was stated:

"It is rare that a management book tells us more than we want to know. But that is the case with *Peanut Butter and Jelly Management,* a kid-inspired manual in a brown paper sleeve."

Since that time, the book has also been published in French and Korean. Just maybe, there is something about the combination of *peanut butter and jelly* and *management* that is as natural to others as it has been to us. And, just maybe, it does translate around the world for both families and business.

CHRIS AND REINA KOMISARJEVSKY
Atlantic Beach, New York

Preface

This is a simple book. It's not theoretical, it's practical. It comes from direct experience. It's about what motivates, what disciplines, what encourages, and what works. And, in particular, what children can teach us about leading adults at work.

This book has one premise: More often than not—if we listen carefully, watch our children attentively at home, see how they behave, and think through how we go about "bringing them up"—we can greatly improve our chances of successfully providing leadership in the workplace.

To our way of thinking, the combination of *peanut butter and jelly* and *management* is as natural to us as . . . well, *peanut butter and jelly*. It provides an immediate link between the hopes, needs, and aspirations of children and those of working adults.

This book started with our six children: Michael, Angelica, James, Nicholas, Matthew, and Stephen. Virtually every day, individually, in pairs, and all together, they bring us opportunities to understand how children learn. In fact, how people of any age learn.

Because they were born only one year apart—today, those six range in age from six to twelve—we quickly became aware that certain behaviors repeated themselves. And we noticed patterns.

But what we learned didn't come only from those six. We had a first child, Christopher Michael. Even though he lived only six months, he taught us how precious life can be and created an emotional bond that lives with all of us every day. And we have three children from a previous marriage—Vera, Katrina, and Ted—who are every bit a part of our family and part of our learning.

Everyone knows that bringing up children takes a lot of understanding and hard work. More often than not, though, what we really need to do is to make a conscious effort to take a deep breath and be patient—and, because we are all far from perfect, work hard at being even more patient than we might have thought possible.

As we talked about how we handled particular situations with our children, we would ask ourselves why we took one particular course of action and not another. Often, we'd wonder aloud whether any approach we took really did have a significant impact. When we pulled back and looked at their actions and ours—as objectively as we could—we could identify those times when we did have a positive impact on their behavior. And when we took the time to look deeply enough, we could begin to understand why.

We then asked ourselves: What lessons were here for us?

What we saw was that each child—every human being—was indeed different. We recognized that each child had special virtues and talents. And, instead of trying to make children—or grown-ups—conform, we should celebrate the variety of their gifts. And learn from them.

The Book Took Shape: At Home . . . at Work

The patterns we saw at home, we began to notice at work.

However, the first few times we noticed parallel behaviors at the office, we didn't really put two and two together. *Then we did.*

Over time, we came to recognize ever more strongly that the issues were often remarkably similar, whether in the concrete and glass office building or in the cedar-sided house.

And so the idea for this book was born. We wanted to share our insights and the connections we made so that leaders might be able to draw on them as they worked to grow their organizations—and themselves.

When we first put pen to paper—or more accurately, fingers to the keyboard—we would write down an incident that happened at home. And, of course, reactions to situations at home tended to be immediate, open, and direct.

In time, the connection to a work situation became clearer. We'd talk about the parallel and write that down, too.

In that way, our book evolved and took on a shape. First, the re-creation of an event at home. Second, what we'd learned from it. And third, the lessons from home which we could apply at work. That became the form which each chapter would take: An experience with our children translated into ideas for leading adults at work.

When we looked at all the chapters together, there were some other important lessons to be learned. Among the most important, we saw that nurturing our children's differences has helped us create a very full and exciting environment in which our family—*as a whole*—can grow.

When we applied the same thinking to the workplace, we saw that different people—with different backgrounds and different skills, but working together as a team—likewise help create a very special environment in a company. An environment that nurtures growth, for the individual employee and for the company as a whole.

When employees thrive, the company can thrive, and become stronger. Build success upon success.

None of the parallels we draw in this book are to imply that the workplace is—or should be—the same as home or that leaders should be paternalistic. Far from it. And certainly we do not mean to imply that employees are children.

Clearly, the home can't provide all the lessons for leadership at work. In fact, there are many to be gleaned from other sources. For instance, there are no insights here about how to read a balance sheet.

It goes without saying that this book never would have been possible without all of our children. Because of them, we saw—and continue to see—things firsthand. As we learn with them, we learn much about ourselves.

In fact, parenting and leading are both works-in-process. They take time, determination, and hard work.

We know we have much yet to learn. No one has all the answers. No one can ever do everything right—at home or at work. But as long as we continue to learn a little more each day, we are going in the right direction.

One thing for sure: Without our children, we would have missed one of the greatest experiences a human being can have—the joy of helping another person learn to stand, to walk, and to run . . . on his own.

Acknowledgments

Thank you—to the many who, in their own special way, helped make this book possible. To all the members of our families who gave us their support.

To Jacquie Flynn who, early on, became very excited about the concept.

To Toby Stein, a superbly talented editor, who was very sensitive to our ideas.

To the many friends of our children who help make their days fun and exciting.

To the teachers of our children who help them learn and grow.

And to the many colleagues at Burson-Marsteller from whom we learn so much.

Thank you.

First String Catcher

Practice, practice, and more practice

At Home . . .

Her long blonde hair was pulled through the opening at the back of the baseball cap, just above the adjustable strap. The hat and the visor were pulled down so far you almost wondered if she could still see. But she knew what she was doing. Besides, if the cap were actually getting in her way, she simply would have taken it off.

Angelica's team this year was the Mets—black shirt with the team name on the front and *Village Cafe* on the back, white baseball pants, the signature royal blue-and-orange NY above the visor on the hat, and, of course, cleats.

Months ago, right before the season started, Angelica had turned ten. When she arrived for her first practice this year, none of the other kids took notice. A lot of girls played Little League. That's the way it should be, of course. If you're good enough, just do it—no matter what.

We think every child should be encouraged to play a team sport. They develop coordination, they learn to try hard, they see what it feels like when everyone plays as a team, they learn what it is like to lose, and they learn what it is like to behave graciously when they win.

All alone, standing at home plate, the kids struggle privately with the pressures of being at bat—the stares of everyone at the game focused directly on them. There's encouragement from the team's parents, but razzing from the other team. Cat-calls from the sidelines. Every now and then, embarrassment of an overzealous Dad. The pressure is enormous. All eyes are on them. Two outs, man on first and third. The score is close. And it's up to them. Only them.

They experience what it is like to play shortstop or play somewhere in the outfield. Then—just when they think the ball will never come their way, their mind wanders, and their attention drifts—they suddenly hear the crack of the bat. It connects. They're startled as the ball climbs and gets closer to them. They look up into the sky, straight into the afternoon sun. But they're too late to judge where the ball is going and the fly ball falls to the ground three yards behind them.

Angelica's coach—his name was Jerry—had made sure from the very beginning that if one of the kids wanted to try playing a certain position, he'd give them that chance. He knew that winning wasn't as important as learning, especially at their age.

We liked that. In our view, he was a great coach. Because he was really *coaching*. Sometimes, other coaches lost sight of what it took to be a coach. They let themselves get too caught up in the game. And whether their team was winning or losing, those others didn't seem to want to let the second-string kids take a try at pitching, catching, or first base—positions that were, they thought, too important. The kids and their desire for a chance unfortunately became secondary.

At home, Angelica would ask Mom to pitch to her. Mom loved sports. She had spent most afternoons as a youngster playing softball, either on the street in front of her house or on one of those concrete playing fields that New York City provided for the neighborhood kids. She was a natural athlete. Her favorite position was shortstop. And she sure *could* catch and throw. When you saw her pull that right arm across her shoulder, you'd better be ready. Her left foot would leave the ground and she'd let the ball fly. You knew it would be hard. Angelica knew that practicing with Mom would be tough. Mom would not ease up. But Angelica also knew that Mom wouldn't criticize when Angelica missed the catch. She'd just simply say, "*Keep your eye on the ball. Try again.*" Mom would throw just as hard the next time. She didn't cut Angelica slack. That would be good, Angelica figured.

Only once did she complain, early in the season. It was all that catcher's equipment that everyone had to share.

"Yuck. This stuff smells," she burst out, when she first put on the chest protector and pulled the catcher's mask down over her face.

The smell didn't faze her for long. Such was her determination.

She was behind home plate now. Crouched down. One knee on the ground. The catcher's mitt in front of her face—not so high that she couldn't see, but not so low that she'd miss giving the pitcher a good target. Her right hand was behind her back, fist clenched in anticipation of the ball being thrown directly at her.

You could hear the sound as the ball smacked into her catcher's glove.

"Ball one," yelled the ump. "One ball, no strikes."

Angelica's right hand quickly came from behind her back and she reached into the mitt to get the ball. She stood up—stretching to the limit every one of her fifty-four inches in height—stepped out with her left foot forward, cocked her arm, and threw the baseball back to the mound.

Angelica returned to her spot behind home plate, knelt down again and got ready. She glanced at the runner on first base. And then looked at the pitcher.

We were standing at the right side of the fence around home plate. Close, but the wire mask still hid much of her. We could hardly see her face. We could just make out her blue eyes, wide with anticipation as she crouched down waiting for the next pitch. We were nervous because we knew she was.

The second pitch went zinging by. It was wild—high, to the right and fast. In one motion, Angelica grabbed the bottom of her face mask with her right hand, pulled it up, tore it off, and threw it to the ground. On her feet, she looked frantically for the ball. It was still bouncing around in the corner.

Quicker than a wish, she ran over, grabbed the ball. Her instincts—and all that practicing—had paid off. She'd figured out where the play would be. The runner had already left first base as soon as the coach had yelled, "Steal! Run! Go to second!"

But he wasn't fast enough. The ball had left Angelica's right hand and was well on its way to second. The runner, tearing toward second, looking straight for the base, only faintly heard his coach yell, "Come back! Back! Back to first!"

The runner sensed he was in trouble. But he wasn't sure what to do. Not sure if he heard his coach right, he continued toward second and decided to slide. His feet slid out from under him. His arms shot into the air. The red dirt from the ball field came up around him.

But the ball was already there.

"Out!" yelled the umpire, leaning slightly back, his hand—fist tight but with the thumb straight up—moving sharply to the right and over his shoulder, in that characteristic baseball motion that all fans know.

This was the play that Angelica had dreamed about. Feared most. This was the one that she had rehearsed over and over in her mind. And this was the one she had practiced by herself, when she thought no one was looking, deciding just how she was going to grab the mask, throw it off, look around and throw to second, just as hard as she could.

Now the one play she had feared most was the one she could be most proud of.

At the Office . . .

There is no question that in sports, both practice and preparedness are essential to success.

But practice is equally essential in business. It may not take the form of throwing a baseball, shooting hoops for hours on end, hitting serves on a tennis court or perfecting your swing from the top deck of a driving range. And it may not take the form of wind sprints, aerobics or lifting weights.

The fact is, though, that no one can be continually successful without some kind of practice. Individuals need to practice—to rehearse. And teams need to practice—to rehearse.

By and large, people won't ever get really good at any kind of activity unless they recognize that they must continue to learn—and practice what they've learned. When a five year-old plays Little League for the first time, he plays tee-ball, where the team uses a ball with a soft cover and a soft inner core. It looks like a regular baseball, but it doesn't hurt as much when the ball slips past the mitt and bounces off an arm or a knee. The point is, that child won't ever get good enough to handle a harder ball if he or she doesn't get outside and work at it. Practice catching. Practice getting under those "high poppers" and catching them before they hit the ground. Or getting in front of the "grounders" so that they don't fly right by.

So it is in business. Practice there may take different forms, but it's no less vital. Practice means being ready— seriously ready. Ready for that presentation. Ready for that speech. Ready to launch that new product. Ready to make that acquisition. Ready to embark on a new strategy. Ready to close down an out-dated plant. Ready to steer the company in a different direction.

Many times, practice takes the form of *mental rehearsal.* Turning something over and over in your mind. Looking at the research. Anticipating difficult moments or tough questions. Playing out all the *what ifs* in your mind.

True. You can never anticipate every situation. But, if you practice, you'll be far better prepared—whatever the situation.

Keep in Mind . . .

Practice may not make perfect. But it often gives the boost to turn good into excellent. As you lead people, encourage them to focus on practice and preparation.

Suggest the following:

❏ *Remember, mental rehearsal is practicing—but inside your mind.* Every world-class athlete runs things through a mental rehearsal before stepping out to compete. The same is true of world-class leaders of businesses, nonprofit organizations, trade associations and other institutions. They, too, mentally rehearse the steps they take to grow their organizations or move them in a new strategic direction.

❏ *Try to imagine all the possibilities and then think through how you might handle each one of them.* Play through a variety of scenarios. Map out in your mind—or, better yet, on paper—what might happen and precisely how you would react. Be thorough. Think of all the possibilities. Write down each action and reaction. Then review them. Improve your responses if they need it.

❏ *Ask others to critique your plans.* This can only strengthen your strategies and add to your conviction—and your persuasiveness. Looking at all the possible options—all the possible reactions—will make your plans more thoughtful and will help you anticipate things that, alone, you might have neglected. As they teach in the military: *The battle is often won or lost before it is ever fought.*

❏ *Be flexible—be ready to react quickly.* The more you practice, the more instinctive your response will be. And primed instincts will serve you well.

❏ *You're the coach—encourage, don't discourage.* Learning—whether in sports or in business—takes time. No one gets it right the first time. You build self-esteem when you take the time to point out what's being done right. And you build perseverance when you point out what's being done wrong and what needs to be done to get it right. Encourage people to think through a task beforehand. And, if something doesn't work the first time, think some more about it and try again.

❏ *Keep the pressure up.* Don't shelter your staff from the pressure of their jobs. Train them well, give them the authority they need, and then let them shoulder the responsibility and the pressure. If you've chosen well—if you've coached well—they will be able to handle it.

❏ *Remember though, there's always a "wild card."* One important point to keep in mind: Regardless of how hard you try to think through each and every scenario, you'll miss at least one. And, chances are, at some time or another—probably more often than you'd like to admit—you will have to deal with a situation you didn't predict. Even in those cases, all your practice will stand you in good stead. You'll be better able to analyze the new situation and more quickly develop an appropriate response.

At the Arrival Gate

Communication opens doors—and people

At Home . . .

Fully loaded, it weighed 125 tons. As the sun bounced off its silver body, there were sudden flashes of light—bright like the sparks that fly from a welder's torch at night when the blue flame melts the solder and fuses the metal. Looking out at the tarmac, you could almost hear the sound as the airplane's ten tires, still hot from landing, ground the loose stones on the asphalt. The rudder moved, the nose wheel started to turn to the left and 155 feet of steel and stretched sheet metal pivoted and followed around. American Airlines flight

833 from Dallas/Fort Worth to New York's LaGuardia airport pulled up to the gate. The blades of the high-pitched turbines whined as they slowly came to a stop. The gangway crawled toward the airplane, extending its neck like a turtle toward the door.

The six kids had been talking about this day for months. Their older sisters and brother were coming for a couple of weeks. Now, the six were looking out the huge airport windows, jumping up and down and waving. The thick glass kept their yells from being heard outside. But, reflected in the window, we could see all those blue eyes, bright with anticipation, darting back and forth, as they tried to catch a glimpse of their siblings inside those tiny airplane windows.

Not right away, but pretty quickly, Angelica realized that they would have to move away from the window and station themselves near the Arrivals door if they wanted to get to Vera, Katrina, and Ted the moment they came out.

"Over here, guys!" yelled Angelica. Her five brothers ran with her. We did our best to catch up—but we knew they wouldn't be going far. We'd all done this before. Many times, in fact. The three older kids from Dad's previous marriage had been coming to visit ever since they could remember. Sometimes, the visits were like this one: in the middle of the summer when school was out and everyone thought about taking vacations. There were many other times, though. And there were those visits in the middle of December when they came east for the holidays. Those stays, in particular, were pretty exciting for the three oldest. That was when they got to leave behind the neither-warm-nor-cold Texas winter and see some snow—if the weather in the northeast cooperated. It was also a time when they might go skiing and try to teach the younger ones what they had learned when *they* were the novices.

Vera was the oldest. She had been born in the hospital at Carswell Air Force Base, just outside Fort Worth. Dad had been a Captain in the Army at that time, recently back from Vietnam and a helicopter instructor pilot at Fort Wolters, the Army helicopter training base— now, long since closed—50 miles west. That had been in the early 70s. Now, Vera was a registered nurse, having put herself through nursing school, working during the day and studying at night. She liked the challenge and the pace of the emergency room and spoke with well-deserved pride of keeping her cool as she stepped forward to examine trauma patients when they were wheeled in on gurneys.

Katrina was four years younger. She'd spent some time as a physical fitness trainer but now worked in a Dallas law firm as a paralegal. She'd gone to school to get her paralegal training and, even now, was thinking of going to law school. At first, none of us believed that this was what she really wanted to do. Yet, as so many kids do, she surprised us.

Their younger brother, Ted, was in college. But studying wasn't his thing. He had turned nineteen earlier in May, and had decided that he wanted to go to work. He told us that he liked music—but we were far from sure that that was the direction he wanted to take professionally. He'd find out—for himself. That's the way it is with your children. You do what you can. You tell them what you think. You support them. But past a certain point, they're on their own.

We called them our three Texas kids. Mom treated them like hers. Often, the six young ones would be asked, *How many brothers and sisters do you have?* And the answer always totaled ten children in the family. None of the kids used the word "half." That wasn't part of our thinking and it wasn't part of theirs. Simply, they were all brothers and sisters.

From the very beginning, it was communication that made the difference. It was tough at first. The kids from Dad's previous marriage couldn't understand the divorce. And that was understandable. It was emotional and difficult for them—were *they* being divorced? That fear was understandable. Allaying it took time. Every aspect of making the transition from old family to new family took time. Lots of it. And there will always be some rough spots. But we talked. We even argued. There were tears. We talked some more. We acknowledged the hurt. But, finally, Dad—and Mom—were blunt about the fact that there was a time to accept things as they were. That way we could, in all honesty, be family for one another.

And we became that. We treated all the kids equally. We encouraged the kids to talk to each other on the phone. We traded photographs. We went to graduations. And we spent time together. In the beginning, when Dad was working in Europe, we went to the Alps, traveled the coast of France, and took a trip to Germany to see the town where Vera had lived when she was a very young girl. Later on, our reunions took us to Washington, D.C., Busch Gardens, and Kings Dominion. Perhaps best of all were those unstructured days spent on the beach together, as a family.

Now, the gangway door opened and the three Texas kids came through, one right after the other, backpack slung over the shoulder and a carry-on grasped by the hand. They'd done this so many times that they knew better than to check luggage. Too many delays and more clothes than they'd really need. So why bother?

The six younger kids broke into a run. You could hear the slap of sneakers as twelve feet hit the floor. Michael, James, and Nicholas were a little more reserved and held back. But the three others had cast themselves in an action movie. And, as soon as they got close enough, Angelica, Matthew, and Stephen seemed to catapult themselves into the air.

The three oldest knew what to expect. Bags dropped

quickly, each reached out to catch one of the younger kids.

Nicholas was a little shy. He sort of turned his face to the side when Katrina reached down to give him a kiss. But that was the way it was with him. He'd warm up pretty fast. For those first few moments, though, he held back a little. Michael was trying to act grown up. James was full of smiles. The three others had found their mark and they were being carried down the airport hallway toward the exit. Mom and Dad had the carry-ons. All the others held hands as we crossed the street to the car in the parking garage.

The talk didn't stop all the way home.

At the Office . . .

Bringing different people together isn't easy. Different backgrounds. Different values. Different emotions. Different goals. Different stages in their lives.

There are countless families in which children of different marriages are brought together, with varying success. It's never a cinch. It wasn't in our family. It isn't in anyone's.

There are countless corporate mergers that try to bring together markedly different companies, with markedly different styles and cultures. These are never simple either.

Most corporate mergers and acquisitions *do not work*. The simple truth is: *Deals are easy to make but hard to make work.*

The new team will rarely be seamless. But the new partnership can work. It can be made to work quite successfully. Sometimes, it can—in time—work wonders.

Still, creating a new team—out of what would otherwise be disparate groups of people—is a daunting task. Needless to say, it takes a lot of work. Perhaps more than anything, it takes a lot of candor and a lot of communication. Both are critical in establishing the framework for success—long before the terms of a merger or acquisition are even put on paper, let alone signed.

The first communications goal is to find common ground. In business the bond is, most likely, one of strategy. Two companies come together in order to help each other fulfill their strategic goals. They might complement one another. One might bring geographic resources. Another might bring technological advances, new products, or an accomplished research capability. Another might bring a specialized and well-trained workforce, coupled with a unique knowledge base. Yet another might bring financial resources or access to capital.

But for a merger or acquisition to be successful, a second key element is necessary: The two companies must have common values. That commonality, too, must be understood and, indeed, reinforced through communication.

There is no substitute for communication when you are bringing two organizations together. And you just can't do too much of it. Consistent, regular communication between leadership at all levels—similar to consistent and regular communication between a Mom or Dad, a step-Mom or step-Dad—will let everyone know what kind of behavior is expected.

And in strong companies—like strong families—straightforward communication reinforces a sense of respect, which in turn encourages people in their differences so they are willing to share their points of view, their insights, and their long-term goals.

These same guidelines for success are vital to any kind of corporate initiative that aims to bring new and different people together, whether through an acquisition or simply by bringing new people into a company. Growing organizations—learning organizations—work hard to create a diverse workforce. In this context, "diversity"—used in the broadest possible sense—is very important.

Quite simply, new people bring with them into a company new talents, new ways of thinking and new ways of doing things. And that is healthy. It creates new opportunities, new business—and growth.

Keep in Mind . . .
As you lead your organization—and as you look to expand by acquiring other organizations or to expand

your workforce by hiring new people—don't lose sight of the following:

❑ *Communicate, communicate, and communicate some more.* As the organization's leader, you must be the most vocal and the most active communicator. Beyond developing strategy and delivering the financial results, a strong leader must be a strong communicator. It is one of your most critical responsibilities. It is just that act of communicating which creates and then strengthens a common bond within an organization and a common direction for its staff.

❑ *Send a consistent message.* You and your team must send consistent messages about the organization, its values, its goals, and what is expected of each member of the larger team. By your words—and, very importantly, your behavior—you create the right kind of environment for success.

❑ *Do it in partnership with key members of your team.* You need their help. You need partners. You need others who "champion" the messages. You need those other people who will communicate when, for some reason, you can't—for example, when you are deeply involved in a meeting halfway around the world. You can't be everywhere at once. These people need to speak the same language as you—with the same passion. In a way, they act as "surrogates" for you. They are "champions," too.

❑ *It's your job.* Those people can help you, but they can't take your place in building a bond with people new to the company. That's your job. You need backup but you alone are the leader. You create the style. You set the tone. You set the values. You lay out what is expected. You lead—the others follow.

❑ *Create the framework for a common bond.* When you first think about acquiring a company, merging with another organization, entering into a strategic partnership, or even combining two departments into one—put down on paper the strategic rationale and then list the three key things you must do in order to make it successful. Go through the thought process of asking yourself, Why? Does it make sense? And follow that with clear thinking about your role in making it work. Write down where you must take the lead. Write down the first things you would say to an assembled group, representing both companies or both organizations. And write down how you want them to behave so that everyone is facing—and moving—in the same direction.

❑ *Give the "new guys" room to grow.* When you bring in new people, don't let them be swamped by cries of "We never did it that way." See to it that they have a voice—a place to go in the organization—so that new ideas can flourish. Don't get discouraged when some of the "old guys" scratch their heads and wonder why that new person was hired. Keep on challenging old ways of thinking.

❑ *Make sure that the "new guys" don't become the "old guys" too soon and fall into the trap of hesitating to do things differently or try out different things.* Put teams together—teams of people who never worked together before but have something to teach one another. Let the pot simmer and see what kind of stew emerges. But, at all times, strengthen the framework for collaboration. And keep your focus on the common bond.

THREE

The Captain and the Goalie

Leaders step forward

At Home . . .

Nicholas was only seven and the skinniest kid on the team. But that didn't seem to matter. And just because the asphalt was hard, that was no excuse. When the street hockey puck came flying at him, he didn't flinch. In fact, he stepped into it, just so that more of the goal would be covered and there would be less chance that the puck could slip by.

The goalie pads came up almost to his waist. The Rollerblades stuck out from beneath the foam. The helmet—the one with the blue and red logo of the New York

Rangers on it—covered his face and his neck. So there was not much for a parent to worry about.

Still, when he stood there and that hard plastic puck came flying, you couldn't help but shudder a bit. He didn't though. He knew what had to be done and he wasn't about to let that puck make it past him.

He stood his ground. Most of the time, he stayed behind the crease. That was where he knew he was supposed to be. But, at other times, his eagerness got the better of him and he couldn't resist skating out with his other teammates as they moved the puck down the street toward the other goal. He was pushing them to score that point. Just by being alongside, he thought he might be able to help get that puck into the net.

Boy, did he ever cheer. He razzed the other team. He heckled the stick handler when he saw him racing down the street with the puck, moving fast toward his goal. He encouraged his own teammates: "Get the puck!" "Don't let him pass!" "Shoot, shoot, get that goal!"

When the other team came flying down looking for the puck that he had just shoved aside with his goalie stick, he stood his ground, his stick back in position in front of his skates. Leaning over—facing the other team head on—once again, his mission was to guard the goal. He looked straight at the other team. No one was going to intimidate him just because they might be bigger or older. Nicholas knew that he could always pick himself up, shake off the hurt, and get right in there again, skating hard and facing that flying puck once more.

Everyone wanted Nicholas on their team. His brothers always wanted him on theirs. They saw themselves together. Like the Florida Panthers, they would say: "Nice guys, tough hockey." Whatever the sport, if they played it together, they played as a team. Well, they were brothers.

When they chose sides, Nicholas was the first picked. In other situations, he was a pretty quiet kid. But, once he had those pads on and that stick clutched tightly in his gloves, he was the one who made things happen. Protecting the goal was his responsibility—he felt he owned it.

Nicholas stepped in to take charge because this was his game. He loved it. He was the team's leader, and everyone knew it. Somehow, *his* team skated faster. *His* teammates didn't tire easily. And they *never* quit.

At the Office . . .
Every organization needs leaders. Someone has to take charge, make decisions, move things forward.

Someone has to *own the goal.*

Whether in sports, in the military, or at the office, leadership is critical to success. Leaders step in and take responsibility. They size up a situation and evaluate the options. Then they act.

There's nothing quite as gratifying as watching a leader emerge in an organization. Sometimes you can be surprised. Leaders come from all sorts of backgrounds.

Their families, their schooling, their work experience, their nationalities, their races are as diverse as America itself.

But there are some shared qualities:

- True leaders are self-confident.
- They lead from up front, not from behind.
- They have self-esteem.
- They are intelligent.
- They can communicate well.
- They work hard and have always worked hard.
- They are passionate about what they are doing.
- They have strong values.
- They are inquisitive and always on the lookout to learn more about almost anything, but especially in their areas of expertise.
- They learn from reading—and they learn from other people.
- They listen.
- They don't hesitate to make decisions but they also encourage others to do the same.
- They are willing to take risks.
- They are respectful of subordinates as well as superiors.
- They engender trust.
- They don't have to yell to get attention.
- They give people a chance to prove themselves by giving them responsibility.
- They believe in the power of people to do the right

thing, to work hard and to create results—they empower others and they cheer them on.
- And they are instinctive people. They trust their instincts. They trust their gut.

No one can ever anticipate all the situations he or she will face or all the decisions that will have to be made at work or, for that matter, at home. There will be many situations no one could have forecast. Indeed, all too often, unanticipated situations need to be faced and addressed very quickly. Emergency or crisis decisions need to be made and made correctly.

Make no mistake, training is very important. So is experience. Knowing what it takes is critical to making the right decision. Whether in sports, the military, at home, or in business, you've got to know what you're doing or else you could make exactly the wrong decision. And in some professions—the military, for example— that could mean the difference between life and death.

Someone has to make the decision and take responsibility. And that's what leaders do.

Real leadership is just that—real. It's not pretend. It's authentic. At the same time, it's modest, simply because leadership means giving others power . . . not keeping it all to yourself.

All organizations need this kind of leadership. You can't have a successful organization without real leadership, without confident people ready to step forward and take responsibility.

Keep in Mind . . .

As you work to create a successful organization, you need always to be on the lookout for the leaders of today and tomorrow. You can't run it on your own. You need help. You need others to work with—you need others to work through to get the job done. And you need to nurture the next generation of leadership.

❑ *Remember, you can't get off the ground without the pilot.* We would all like to lead by consensus and get agreement from everyone. But that's just not possible. Organizations need a leader. Someone has to make the decisions, get things going. Provide direction. Act.

❑ *Keep in mind that we all will be judged by our courage.* Leaders take chances—and risks. They lead from up front, not from behind. They encourage looking at things differently, and they embrace change. No successful general, no successful business leader shies from doing things that are bold and different.

❑ *Think about what might be called the "vacuum philosophy."* Leaders don't hesitate to step in and take charge. If something needs to get done, watch to see who it is that steps forward. Some people are naturally courageous. Maybe they have an extra gene for leadership. They're the ones who don't shy away from a challenging situation; instead they take it on— sometimes to test themselves, other times simply because they know that it needs to be done. Authority and power will go to the individual who steps into the vacuum, takes responsibility, and accepts the challenge of getting the job done.

❏ *Build a team of leaders.* Create a culture where leadership, taking responsibility, and stretching oneself are recognized and rewarded. Every organization has its own culture. Yours should be one where stepping out from the crowd and doing more are prized behaviors. Find innovative ways to reward those potential leaders. And put leaders in touch with other leaders so that they learn from each other.

❏ *Be on the lookout for those who really do want to "own the goal."* Try to identify those who take that responsibility to heart—and will be accountable for their actions regardless of the outcome.

❏ *On the next resume you get, look to see if the candidate has worked since high school.* Initiative and a willingness to work hard show up early in life. Someone who decided to work summers while going to school—and has worked ever since—clearly is worth talking to. That kind of energy and dedication probably carried forward, even if he or she didn't go to the most prestigious university in the country.

❏ *Check out those with military experience.* The military is an extraordinary training ground for future leaders. Serving in the armed forces—even in times when there is no war—forces young people to perform some tough leadership tasks and take on more responsibility at an early age than they would ever have to in civilian life. In the military most young men and women mature more quickly. They learn self-discipline. They learn respect. And they prove to themselves that they can accomplish a lot—even more than they might have anticipated—simply because they put their minds to it. Historians tell us that the most productive group of college students in the history of this country was the generation that came home from the military when the Second World War came to an end. They had the best grades in college and went on to be, perhaps, the most extraordinary generation in our country's history.

FOUR

Brothers and Sisters Stick Together

Teamwork works

At Home . . .

It started out like most other days. Each of the children woke up at a slightly different time, except for Matthew and Stephen who came downstairs together. And last. They were the slowest to get going— but, then again, they were the last to go to bed. You could hardly get them to lie still at night, let alone close their eyes when it was time to go to sleep. It's funny how that surge of energy always seemed to come just when the lights were turned off.

But now it was morning. Bare feet running on the kitchen tile. One walking slowly and scuffling his feet as he looked out of the corner of his eye just to make sure you really noticed how difficult it was for him to make it downstairs.

Still, the morning was getting started. Cereal for some. Waffles for others, with lots of butter and syrup, and occasionally scrambled eggs with bacon and toast. More choices because it was Saturday. As it sank in what day it was, they started to think about what they wanted to do. You could almost see their excitement building. Some were ready for showers, others ran down to play Sony Playstation or a game on the computer. Angelica went straight for the phone to call her friends and plan when they would be getting together. It was outside with the Rollerblades and hockey sticks for the older boys.

Nonstop play was their agenda for the day. Balls, bats, Rollerblades, gloves, sticks, pucks, goalie pads, nets, and tennis balls—everything pulled out, maybe to be used, maybe not. But thrown around, nonetheless.

The day went quickly. The play never stopped, except for a few moments taken out for a quick drink and a peanut butter 'n jelly sandwich. And then, of course, some kind of snack as the day wore on.

But as the daylight began to fade, we knew it was getting closer and closer to the time when the kids had to go inside, clean up, have some supper and begin to quiet down for the night.

We knew we'd have to remind them a few times: "Hey, guys, let's get things put away and clean up the garage."

That was the last thing on their minds. The protests began . . . moans, groans, and seemingly desperate cries of "But I'm too tired."

And they really were tired. Like many a protest, of course, theirs might have been a little overdone, a little melodramatic, a little too much. But, then again, almost an entire day passing the puck back and forth and racing up and down the street on Rollerblades uses up a lot of energy. There's no doubt they felt genuine fatigue.

Yet they knew they didn't have much choice. They had a job to do. They might have to be reminded a couple of times, but it wasn't too long before they realized that all the protests in the world wouldn't change the fact that the sticks, the pucks, and the goalie helmets needed to be put away and the garage cleaned before the sun went down. And dusk was quickly approaching.

Slowly, the oldest, Michael, grabbed some of the sticks and worked his way up the driveway toward the garage.

"Hey!" he yelled. "You guys need to help. Come on."

The protests gradually wound down. James grabbed the net. Nicholas went to find some of the hockey pucks that had been sent skidding to the far reaches of the street with many a loud slap shot. And Matthew, trying to convince us that he had absolutely no strength left, crawled toward the garage on his hands and knees.

Slowly, but with growing willingness, they became a different kind of team. With a job to be done and a part for everyone to play.

There's always been teamwork in our family. With ten kids, it's essential.

But it was at day camp during the summers that they had also learned the importance of helping each other out. They all went to Twin Oaks, where the owners took great pride in creating an atmosphere of respect and caring. As a result, the counselors looked out for the kids, the kids responded by looking out for each other, and, if something needed to be done, everyone pitched in. That was how it was done. Period.

Now, as the sun was sinking lower in the sky, the kids intuitively apportioned the tasks. Michael took the broom off the hook. James tossed the skates in the storage box and went to get the dustpan. Nicholas walked to the edge of the yard, looking for balls that had been hit astray. Matthew and Stephen wheeled their bikes to the back of the house.

Angelica—with her friends Marisa, Blake, Jackie, and Danielle—were down the street listening to their favorite CDs and choreographing their own dances. We could see her dancing on the grass only two houses away and we called out to her to come home. After delaying a little by playing just one more song, she wandered back, put her CD player in her room and came back out again to lend a hand.

Nicholas came up with some pucks and an armful of tennis balls, newly discovered among the bushes. He went straight to the battered laundry detergent bucket and threw them in with the baseballs. He took his turn at sweeping. The broom was twice his size and hardly manageable, but he gave it a try and some of the sand and dirt made it into the garbage can.

Together, they put away all those toys, bikes, and equipment, and swept the garage clean in record time—much faster than if one had tried to do it alone.

At the Office . . .

Teamwork—there's nothing quite like it. Under the most demanding of circumstances, when everyone seems to be too tired to go on, unappealing tasks and even those which might seem otherwise insurmountable can be tackled successfully.

The power of people operating as a team—with trust and partnership—is remarkable. Many people first think of sports when they think of teams, but successful businesses are invariably made up of successful teams.

In business, each individual has a special role to play. It might involve a particular skill, or a unique professional experience. It might capitalize on specialized training. By itself, each role is valuable—but when part of a team effort, it is far more powerful. In fact, its effectiveness is multiplied. Individual strengths, coupled with a strong sense of teamwork, are what make a company successful.

Like the best sports teams, the best companies know that, if they nurture teamwork, they will be able to accomplish far more than otherwise. There is something almost magical that happens when a group of people get together to tackle a task as a team. The thinking is more thorough, the solutions are more creative, and that spirit of teamwork is a powerful drive for convincing the team members to watch out for each other and help overcome any difficulties that another employee might be facing.

Creating success in business requires a seamless approach to challenges and opportunities. That means fostering a common bond and a common goal. It means celebrating teamwork.

Keep in Mind . . .
It is your task to build the team. The power of an individual is exponentially greater when he or she works as part of a team. The ideas are richer, the solutions more varied, and the perspectives much broader. That partnership—like linked hands creating a bridge—is far stronger than any collection of individuals at dealing with problems and taking advantage of opportunities.

To build a strong team, do the following:

❏ *Focus on teams rather than "stars."* Most leaders today don't want their company to be dependent on "stars." Stars come and go. They can hold you hostage and they rarely mentor others because they are fearful of losing even an inch of their exalted ground to an apt student, especially one who has the potential to be their successor. Stars feel threatened. Team members feel *enriched* by the opportunity to collaborate.

❏ *Be a teammate yourself.* If you really want to build a team, your own sense of team spirit must be genuine. If you're not really committed to working collaboratively, everyone will know it and you will fail. Don't try to fake it. It won't work. Start by making sure that you haven't put a star on your own door.

❏ *Develop a framework of trust.* Trust is key. Without it, there can be no team.

❏ *Create common objectives.* If you want to build a real team, make sure that everyone has specific business objectives to meet. These drive behavior to achieve common goals.

❏ *The team will become stronger because of the individual, while the individual will be able to accomplish more because of the support of the team.* Without the particular contributions of individuals, the team is nothing. At the same time, each individual will gain from belonging to the team. So don't hesitate to single out those who make a difference to the team. A strong team will have the confidence to applaud individual accomplishments.

❑ *Think of yourself as a teacher.* The truth is, you are. If you want to develop teamwork, you need to do it with patience, understanding, discipline—and you need to use everything *you* learn. Quote what others say, in other disciplines and other industries. There are plenty of lessons there for you to pass on. They come from history, from world leaders, from corporate chief executives, from the military, from religion, from adventurers, and, of course, from sports. Examples from other walks of life can be very powerful teaching tools.

❑ *Create a dialogue, invite other points of view, accept criticism, and when it comes, don't take it personally.* If you want to create a sense of teamwork, you have to get a genuine dialogue started. In the conference room or at a team dinner, talk about the issues openly. Encourage members of the team to speak out. The rule is: Be respectful, but say what's on your mind. This certainly involves some risk. Ideas may be put forward that, for some reason, cannot be acted upon. Still, everyone wants to know that their viewpoint is listened to and respected, even if the final decision does not exactly match the one they would have made on their own. There is also the risk that you, the team leader, will be criticized. That's part of the dialogue process. The key is to be open, let others express their opinions, while you remain objective. Listen to what's said and evaluate it honestly. Accept valid criticism and learn from it. Put the rest aside. And then be ready to act. Move on with sensible, practical decisions which are in the best interests of the team and the company.

❏ *Use your incentive compensation plan to reinforce everyone's responsibility in helping to reach the organization's goals.* Make sure that the objectives in your incentive compensation plan are all built on a common strategy, and be sure that they stress teamwork. They can be powerful bonding tools. Use them wisely to develop priorities and to create common performance objectives.

❏ *Never stop talking about teams.* Keep talking that way, no matter what. Even when it seems that people just don't get it and it appears to be taking too long for a real partnership to develop, don't give up. If you create an atmosphere conducive to teamwork, it will happen. When it does, make sure *you* celebrate the team.

FIVE

Balloons for Christopher Michael

An emotional bond

At Home . . .

The sky was a piercing blue. It seemed to go on forever, deep into the atmosphere, without a break. Not a single cloud. In the mountains, the bright sun reflected off the deep snow—so sharp it hurt your eyes. It was March, thirteen years ago. The place was Verbier, the skiing village high in the Swiss Alps. Just over the peak, across the Grande Saint Bernard pass, was Italy.

There were six of us in the car. It was one of those large BMWs. Mom and Dad in the front, Dad driving. Vera, Katrina, and Ted in the back seat. Vera, the oldest, was holding Christopher Michael on her lap. He was just six months old. He was our—Reina and Chris's—firstborn child. And this was our second wedding anniversary.

The older kids had come from Texas to be with us during the winter school break. That was one of our special holidays together. We'd decided to take them skiing. This time of the year, there was always plenty of snow and the weather was starting to warm up. It promised to be a great experience for everyone.

Especially for Christopher. At that time, we were living in an apartment in Switzerland, and the winters by Lake Geneva—where work had taken us to live for four years—tended to be overcast and damp. The Swiss had a name for the wind that came across the lake in January and February—they called it, the *Bise*. And it was a biting cold. So, it was good to get Christopher out of our apartment in Geneva and into the warmer weather and sunshine of the mountains.

When Christopher was born, Mom almost died. We'll never know exactly what happened. Later on, there would be a lot of debate among the doctors, too many meetings to discuss what might have gone wrong. But at the time, one thing was clear: The bleeding just wouldn't stop. Mom needed tremendous amounts of blood. Even as the transfusions were taking place, the speeding ambulance transported her from a private hospital to the Cantonal hospital in Geneva where she was met by a trauma team of a dozen doctors who operated on her well into the night. The head obstetrician at the Cantonal hospital that day was our hero. He saved her life. But, to this day, ambulances racing down the street with lights flashing and sirens wailing remind us of that terrifying day.

There were difficulties with Christopher, too. His muscles didn't have the strength they should. He couldn't hold his head upright. His little hands were always clenched in a fist. He couldn't stretch his legs or raise his arms above his shoulders. Something was wrong. Again, we didn't know what. *How could a pregnancy that had seemed entirely normal culminate in so much being amiss?*

Grandma—Mom's mother—came and stayed for almost two months, giving so much of the emotional and physical support that was needed.

She would have stayed longer. She gave Mom every bit of energy she had.

We all went to the hospital every day. It was hard. Very hard. We believed from the beginning that, whatever happened, it was God's will. But we were frightened. We both prayed hard for our son. We cried, too. We wanted Christopher well—and home with us.

After three months in the hospital, Christopher finally did come home. Mom spent every waking moment with him. She took him to specialists. She rocked him. Held him. Massaged him. Talked to him. *Loved him.* And devoted herself to doing whatever she could in the hopes that he would get better. She cried, but she never stopped trying.

From the very beginning, Dr. Pierre Klauser, Christopher's pediatrician, tried to keep us hopeful that Christopher would somehow develop and gain the strength he needed. But we distinctly heard the concern in Doctor Klauser's voice when he would wonder aloud why Christopher hadn't smiled yet. He didn't have those involuntary smiles that most infants have—it's what the Swiss call *smiling to the angels*. Christopher didn't do that.

We thought, *Maybe in the Swiss mountains, with his brother and sisters giving him so much playful attention, he'll finally smile.*

The road to Verbier wound back and forth up the mountain. It had been a long journey, but late that afternoon we reached our hotel. We'd rented a place close enough to the base of the gondolas so that the kids wouldn't have to lug their skis too far each morning.

But we never got a chance to ski that March.

Christopher died early that evening.

We tried everything to get him to start breathing again. Mouth-to-mouth, and when that had no effect, we ran with him in our arms, screaming, to find the local doctor. The doctor tried to bring him back to life. But it was God's decision—not ours. Life's so fragile. In the space of only a few moments, Christopher was gone. So much of it is still a blur.

We all flew back to the States right away. We wanted Christopher to be buried where our families were. In fact, he would be buried next to his Grandpa—Mom's Dad.

Christopher never had a chance to meet Grandpa—who had died a few years before—but it always seemed to us as though they would have had a lot in common.

Rob, the funeral director, volunteered all the funeral arrangements back in the States. About his fee, quite simply, he said, "I would never take a penny . . . not on the death of a baby."

Dad asked Rob if he could go with him to pick up the coffin when it arrived by Swissair. He answered that it wasn't really necessary—he was probably just trying to be kind. But Dad insisted. He wanted to be there. At about two in the morning, Dad and Rob drove to the hangar in the cargo holding area at Kennedy airport. The night was dark and cold. The room, so big, so impersonal. The ceilings, improbably high, with cartons piled way up. The coffin was so small. It didn't weigh much at all. It was so tiny. *How could our baby be in there?* And then, the hearse seemed so big. It just wasn't fair.

The day Christopher was buried at Holy Rood in Westbury on Long Island was cold—but the sun was out and there were family and friends all around.

Michael, Angelica, James, Nicholas, Matthew, and Stephen all know about their brother. They call his gravesite "Christopher's garden." And all five of the boys have Christopher as their middle name in memory of the brother none of them had a chance to know. In fact, if anyone asks Angelica, *How many brothers do you have,* she'll always include Christopher, *"my brother in*

her reply. He is part of our family. He always
will be.

Every September tenth, Christopher's birthday, all
the kids gather in the front of our house, with bunches of
balloons in their hands. All at the same time, they open
their fingers and let the balloons fly. As the balloons float
upwards and catch the wind, the kids yell out as loudly as
they can, "Happy birthday, Christopher!"

Surely, he hears them.

At the Office . . .

Emotions fill our lives every day. We laugh. We cry. We
get angry. We are motivated. We feel discouraged. We are
inspired. We become excited.

Emotions are part of us. They can lift us up. They
can bring us down. But perhaps most important, they
give us a personal framework for what we do and how we
do it.

That's true in the home. Christopher's life—short as
it was—has given a special context to our lives and to the
lives of our children, all of them. The three oldest children witnessed one of the most tragic events that anyone
can face: the loss of a child and the inability of parents to
do anything about it, no matter how hard they try. For all
of us, the loss of Christopher was traumatic. Our sense of
helplessness was also traumatic. But our sense of family

became even stronger than before. And we learned never—never—to take anything for granted.

Six children later, the memory of Christopher lives on, an integral part of our family's life. An emotional bond. And we have created a tradition—those balloons to Christopher—which serve as a special reminder not only of what he left us, but also, and just as important, that he continues to watch over his brothers and sisters.

Just as emotions have a powerful impact at home, they also do at work, although in a very different way. The caution is that companies and other organizations can be very cruel. They can be heartless. Some can be so financially driven that they lose sight of the human element so critical to business success. Without emotion—without that human element—organizations can be successful, but the question is, *How long will they endure?*

Businesses—like people and families—need an emotional bond. They need successes, but they also need failures. They need traditions. They need heroes. They need respect for their founders and founding principles. And they need people of varied talents who personify the very values that have made the company great.

The challenge for a leader in business is twofold. First, to find a way to balance the human and the financial responsibilities. And, second, to create a culture where emotion is fostered in order to help drive the business forward.

Emotion binds people together equally in those times when there is great success and during those times which challenge the economic growth—even the very survival—of the company.

Keep in Mind . . .

As you build your organization, remember that you create the culture of the company. You are the living embodiment of the values you want the organization to have and the values you want everyone to share.

You create the emotional bond which holds your organization together and helps drive success. Think about the following ways you might do it:

❏ *Create an emotional framework.* Emotions alone won't create success. But they create a bond that encourages people to work harder, believe more and take charge of the future. Think of your company or organization—the kind you want to build—in emotional terms. What kind of feel to the organization do you want? What are the primary emotions you want your people to carry with them? What do you think are the emotions that—in your industry—will put you head and shoulders above the competition? Encourage pride and a winning attitude. Encourage a passion for "doing it right."

❏ *Find people in your organization today who embody those emotions.* Build organizational change programs which put the spotlight on them as a means of encouraging others to emulate that kind of behavior. Give those people an opportunity to shine. Ask them to talk about what they do and why they do it. When they talk, their passion—their emotions—will shine through. Expose them to others. Passion and emotions are contagious.

❏ *Institutionalize traditions—or create new ones—which have a strong emotional component.* Celebrate commitment. Celebrate loyalty. Celebrate how much people care about the organization. Thank your staff not only for creating success but thank them for how much of themselves they give to the company each day.

❏ *Don't allow yourself to be shy of emotion.* Let your staff see and feel your emotions. Emotions are not a sign of weakness but rather a sign of strength. Let them know how you feel. Let them hear it in your voice and the way you talk about the business, about your customers, about your successes, and about your failures. People respond to people who have emotions—simply because it is a reminder that they, too, are human.

❏ *Show your emotions but don't let your emotions cloud your judgment.* Your staff should know that you care—care deeply—but they should also know that you will be very objective when decisions need to be made and action needs to be taken.

A Shoe Box under the Bed

Think personal

At Home . . .

It was a shoe box. Cardboard, as you'd expect. But, other than that, it was very special. It had two small hinges on one side and a little clasp on the other. There were splashes of bright green, blue, and yellow on the top and the sides, sort of like a jungle with some trees, sky, and birds.

Five weeks earlier, that same box held a brand new pair of high-tops, a child's size two. Now the wrapping paper had been thrown away and shoelaces pulled through each one of the sixteen loops. Those sneakers had already lost their brand-new sheen. The toes were scuffed, the plastic tips on the laces split and frayed, and mud had days ago dried between the ripples of the rubber soles.

But the box! That was another matter. It belonged to James, who had turned eight just as that summer began. Those sneakers were one of his birthday presents. He liked the sneakers but he *treasured* the box. He had written his name on the outside. And right after his name, he'd put only one word—MINE—in block letters. Pretty large ones, in fact. That way, no one could possibly miss whose box it was. It was his and only his. Every night, just before the lights were turned out, he reached under his bed, pulled it out and lovingly took his own inventory of the contents yet again.

James' box contained all sorts of things. Their only common element was their value to *him*: a few baseball cards—only his favorites, of course. At least two from the New York Mets, the only team for him. There were cards of hockey players—three from the Rangers, of course, plus some from the Panthers. The names were ones almost everyone would recognize and, if you didn't, obviously you didn't know too much about hockey.

And then there were some different-colored marbles, along with candies James thought were really good— Warheads, Lifesavers, and almost any kind which came individually wrapped.

There also was the "diamond" from his trip to Canada. That stone was taken out and turned over in his hands every single night. It shone better than a star. It came from the planetarium in Montreal, so it was precious indeed. Standing in front of the gift shop counter, James had spent fifteen minutes deciding which one was best. He paid for it with his own money, some of the allowance he'd earned by making his bed, putting his clothes away, and doing other chores to help around the house.

Alongside those treasures were some pictures of his brothers and his sister, all together at a farm for apple picking, plus one of him all alone trying to brave the surf on a summer's day. A plastic key was there—from the hotel where he stayed on the trip to Binghamton to visit his cousin in college. And the well-thumbed ticket from last summer's trip to Shea Stadium to see the Mets and the Yankees play in the series which gives the winning team the bragging rights for New York City. There was the writing journal that Mr. Hoffman, his third grade teacher, had given each of his students during the school year. And there were a few pencils, along with an extra eraser—just in case he needed it. He had even hidden some empty candy wrappers in there so Mom and Dad wouldn't find them.

He would sit on his bed, his back to the door, and carefully take everything out to look at it closely. Then, when the time rolled around to turn off the lights, he'd wait until the last moment, put things gently back, close the lid, flip the clasp down and slide the shoe box back under the bed for safekeeping. Until the next night.

At the Office . . .

Cubicle or paneled office, small or large, personal space is very important. It's a little bit of privacy, a little piece of home. That space contains reminders of family and friends, glimpses of special moments, and memories.

Whether at home or at the office, these things nourish the soul. They remind us that work is important but it isn't everything. Pictures and mementos help us keep balance in our lives and, every so often, yank us back to reality when we may have strayed too far or fallen prey to a surge of personal power or overwhelming ambition.

In the case of James, he had his own personal space—that shoe box under the bed. He was not trying to hide it. He was just keeping it close by.

In that same way, it is a healthy sign when your employees decorate their office with reminders of their other, more personal life. They actually might be planning to stay for a while.

We should encourage this personalizing of "their" space. They are settling in and creating an area, however small it may be, which they can call their own. Photographs are pinned on cork boards, others in frames sit on desks, shelves, and credenzas. And that award or special plaque gets hung on the wall. It's personal pride and a tribute to a professional task well done.

Others notice, start a conversation, ask about the people in those pictures, and a different sort of relationship begins. A little more trust develops and there begins to be a stronger connection, a basis on which to relate. With time, this connection grows and allows the team to work better together, helping each other get through the rough spots and the demands of the moment.

From a different perspective, personal space provides another set of clues. If we are really paying attention, it speaks clearly about priorities and opens a window into a colleague's life, giving us a glimpse of the whole person. We just have to *see*.

Leaders need to look closely so that they can better understand the kinds of things that are important to employees. They can use this understanding to put into place the kinds of human resource programs that best meet the needs of their employees.

People give us clues on how we can help them live up to their potential. They also give us clues about the kind of support the organization should be providing them so that they will stay and have a satisfying, productive career.

Keep in Mind . . .
As employers, we should encourage our staff to bring a little bit of their personal life to work. It encourages balance in their lives and that makes the work environment that much more productive and satisfying. Equally important—if we are really paying attention—it also gives us very valuable insights into what new things we

should be thinking about in order to attract and keep the best people we can find. Here are some thoughts:

❏ *Take the time to get to know your staff.* In the rush of our day-to-day jobs, it's often tough to find the time, but we must. Walk around. Talk to people. Relating on a personal level gives us insights into our staff, and these insights can often make the difference between motivating success and permitting failure. Walk the halls regularly.

❏ *Ask about the things you see displayed in employees' offices or at their workstation.* Your interest will be noticed and appreciated. Your staff will see you as a leader who cares.

❏ *Don't be nosy, but be genuinely interested.* Let everyone know that you are interested in how they are. Have a genuine conversation, even if it has to be brief. Ask if they enjoy their work. Ask them for their ideas. Ask them what could be done better. Pay attention to what they say. You will learn more by listening to them than you might through your normal reporting channels. Encourage them to be open. And do it in a friendly yet businesslike way.

❏ *When you visit another location where your organization has an office or a facility, take the time to walk around and say hello to people.* Walk around by yourself. Resist the courteous offers of the office manager or the plant manager to take you around. Go by yourself. Stop by, shake hands, and say hello to everyone, from the support and administrative staff to the people in the mailroom or in shipping and receiving. You will get a pretty accurate feel for the place—you will *sense* the morale there—and you'll have a chance to judge for yourself how things are done.

❏ *Reach out to your employees in some kind of personal way.* Send a "welcome" letter to each new employee the very first day he arrives at work. Send flowers to your staff on the first day of spring to thank them for their hard work and to encourage creativity and new ideas. Send small "thank you" gifts to your administrative and support staff to celebrate those in the company who are all too often ignored amidst the pressures and haste of everyday work. Reach out in some way that is personal, from you to them.

❏ *Create opportunities for your employees to get together socially.* An informal dinner. The after-work social hour. A summer outing for employees and their families. A birthday party or the celebration of an employee's anniversary with the company.

❏ *Encourage work/family initiatives that give people the opportunity to spend more time at home and even work from there, especially if they have young children or need to care for elderly parents.* People have personal issues to attend to. If you give them the opportunity to do so, you will generate extraordinary loyalty. Obviously, not everyone can work from home all the time. And some companies may not even be able to let people do it at all. But be sensitive and responsive when the need is there. Put into place programs that permit your staff to better balance their work and family lives. There might be things you can let them do, such as telecommute, work from home one or two days a week, job share, or take home leave to care for a spouse, child, or other family member who is ill. Look into agencies that will help with elder care or provide "concierge" services for employees. Create ways that employees can use the Internet at work to shop for groceries and other needed items. Survey your employees and find out what they would like to have. And, then, experiment to see what is realistic and if it can work out. Progressive companies—of today and tomorrow—are doing just that. And you don't want to be left behind.

SEVEN

To Grandma's House We Go

Values are palpable

At Home . . .

All the kids knew they would be getting up early that Saturday morning. One by one, they got into the shower, dried off, brushed their teeth, and got dressed. It never went too smoothly, but it did seem to go pretty quickly this time. For one thing, Mom had put their clothes out the night before so there wouldn't be any of those prolonged discussions—sometimes arguments—about what to wear.

They were excited. Happy anticipation. That was their usual reaction when they knew they were going to see Dad's Mom and step-Dad—the kids call her Grandma and him Pop Pop. Six bright faces in the early morning. But experience had given us a clue to what could happen during a two-hour drive. The Caravan with the "turtle top" helped a lot, with the television and video player installed. They could watch one tape and a little bit of another. That kept them somewhat quiet, and sure enough, the two hours went by pretty quickly.

As usual, Grandma was at the front door with a smile to welcome us all. As soon as we walked inside, we noticed that the house smelled of fresh baked chocolate chip cake. The kids knew that she would also have at least three different flavors of ice cream for their visit.

After saying "Hi' to Grandma, they ran into the big room that she used as a dance studio. Tall windows on either side, a big fieldstone fireplace at one end, and a ceiling so high it seemed to rise right past the rafters and straight through the skylights to touch the sun.

Because it was summer, Pop Pop was sitting outside on the deck with a book in his hand. Sometimes, in the warmth of the sun, his eyelids would get heavy. He'd gradually drift off to sleep and the book would slip from his hand, falling to the deck. This year, John Chamberlain would turn ninety. But even though his naps were a little deeper and his breathing a little heavier, once he awoke you could see that his blue eyes were as clear as ever.

The kids always marveled at how thick the books were that he read. They would stare at the hundreds upon hundreds stacked on his ceiling-high bookshelves. And, invariably, one of them would ask—yet again: "Pop Pop, did you really read all those books?" And when he would smile and say he had indeed, their eyes would widen in awe of such an accomplishment. So *many* books. Not their kind of authors though—no Dr. Seuss or Beatrix Potter here—but heavy volumes by authors whose unknown names they would slowly try to pronounce, like John Dos Passos and John Steinbeck. There were also many histories and essays about early America, including his own books, especially the one about *The Enterprising Americans.*

Pop Pop listened. Even with children, he instinctively used that journalist's trick of creating moments when nothing was said just so the other person would chime in with a thought or two. And he'd pay attention to what was said in that moment because it might be an opening to something very important.

For decades, he communicated through the keys of a chipped Smith Corona typewriter, hunting and pecking his way to 700 words each day. He was a writer—a columnist in fact—who saw *everything* and had written his newspaper column, *These Days*, about the changes taking place all around us.

Grandma was dramatic. Full of emotion. She talked about her love for music and dance. She had this great smile that was like an embrace, and her eyes were vibrant as she explained just exactly how to do those very same exercises she taught the many students in her dancing school. Today, floor stretches and leap-swing-slides were fun, and so was marching to the beat of the drum she banged to keep time. Truth to tell, she *always* made the movements exciting. And the laughter of the kids, as they tried and tried to get them right, filled the room to the point of bursting.

Modern dance had always been her life. As Ernestine Stodelle, she had danced with Doris Humphrey, and José Limón. Afterward, it was her own school which gave her the most pleasure—helping young people discover the joys of expressing oneself through movement. Through that school, she was able to keep alive many of the early modern dances which would otherwise have been lost since, of course, there were no video cameras in the 1920s and the 1930s. In fact, scholars from colleges and universities, as well as dance historians, would come with their tape recorders and video cameras and ask her to re-create some of those dances for them so that a record of their choreography would exist. In this way, the great dances of past decades could be performed for new audiences and inspire young choreographers.

To our amazement, the children always seemed to know what was important to Pop Pop and what was important to Grandma. When they were there, they always finished what was on their plates because they could just *feel* how important it was to Pop Pop not to waste food. And when he took them out to the small garden he kept by the side of the road and gently weeded between the budding plants, they always agreed that they, too, could hear the corn and the sunflowers growing.

No one had to tell them to be still and listen carefully as Pop Pop told them how he spent a summer working on a mule boat as it crossed the Atlantic. When, all caught up, they begged for another story, he told about standing for hours, leaned over, packing oranges beneath the California sun . . . bending and leaning, bending and leaning, for long hours in the heat. As you listened you knew that Pop Pop thought that kind of a job was good for a young man—it didn't break your back, it strengthened it.

Later they sat on the floor doing exercises with Grandma. They laughed when she joked with them. But they quickly quieted down and paid really close attention as she spoke slowly from her heart. She was full of life and energy, recounting what it was like to face the lights and feel the movements come from deep in her soul as she danced on stage, helping to make history in those early years. Somehow, they understood that dance and now teaching were her life—and the magical moments she painted left them wide-eyed.

And us, as well. Because in those stories from Grandma and Pop Pop, we too could feel what it was to believe strongly in something. For them it was writing and history and gardening and dancing. We could *feel* the strength it gave, the joy it brought, the precious center it created that could withstand all the pressures the world brought to bear.

At the Office . . .

Values are palpable. Even the youngest children feel them. They instinctively just *know.*

It is these values, passed from generation to generation in the family, which endure. When many of us look back on our childhood, of course, we remember things that we did—where we went on vacation, events at school, the friends we made, the challenges we encountered—but we also remember simply what it felt like to be part of our own family.

What we *felt* were the values that sustained our family. Most of the time, if we really paid attention, we intuited what was important. Of course, sometimes we had to be reminded. And yes, there were times when we had to have a value explained to us. At times, we may have wanted to ignore those traditions that felt constraining to us. But we always *knew.*

In much the same way, we *feel* the values that hold together the fabric of a company.

And in successful companies, that feeling is strong.

In some cases, a company may have a credo, mission statement or statement of values that serves as the underpinning of what the company stands for and how it will behave. If the actions of corporate leadership reflect the credo, it will be credible—it will provide guideposts—and it will endure.

Some companies have founders who are still leading the organization, and their actions form a cumulative record of what that company believes and the values it stands for.

In other companies, the founders are still active even though they may not be making the day-to-day decisions. Yet their very presence and support of the decisions being made help to reinforce the values of the company—which may have been conceived decades earlier but continue to hold together the fabric of the organization.

In many cases there is no written credo and perhaps no founder still involved in the company. The company has become an institution. Indeed, there may have been many chief executives over the years. Still, a system of values is just as important to the fabric of the company.

In this situation, it is the leader—by his or her actions, tone and very style—who sets the values and constructs the framework for how decisions will be made.

There is the potent scent of truth in the old Italian saying: *The fish rots from the head.*

The leader—and by extension the rest of the leadership team—is the keeper of the culture and the reputation of a company. It is an awesome responsibility. In many circumstances, it is a strong value system, a discernibly strong moral culture that will determine a company's reputation—and help deliver strong financial results, even in difficult times.

Behavior communicates values best. Meetings, speeches, credos, and written statements of values are all very helpful to reinforce and clarify, but people believe what they experience far more than what they are told.

A company's reputation, like its culture, is built on the foundation of what people actually see—and feel—happening. That starts at the top. The leader's actions must be based on solid values. And when that happens, those values will be felt throughout the organization—and the company's entire business world.

Keep in Mind . . .

In a leadership role, you need to devote some time to think about the values that you want the organization to have. Those values will help you attract the right people. They will help you weather the crises that you will undoubtedly face at various times. They will help you attract and keep valued customers. And they will help you maintain a loyal shareholder base even when revenues and earnings move up or down for reasons beyond your control. In short, they will help create your success. Think about the following:

❏ *Never forget: You are responsible for the culture and the reputation of the organization you run.* Even if you don't want the responsibility, you've got it. According to research among key opinion leaders, forty percent of the reputation and value of a corporation depends *directly* on the reputation of the chief executive.

❏ *Emphasize values and let people know what is important.* The same way you set the tone, you set the values: by your actions. That's the main way you determine the culture of the company. Leaders lead by example.

❏ *Draft your own credo—even if you never publish it.* Try putting down on paper at least five behaviors—values—that you think are most important to the growth and prosperity of your company. Then take some time to ask yourself: Can you personally live up to that expectation? Can the organization? What do you have to do each day to make sure?

❏ *Take the time to explain why you make certain decisions.* Talk about what you did and *why*. Give your staff the benefit of your insights. Discuss your priorities. Invite questions.

❏ *Do right.* Most people really want to do what is right, rather than what is expeditious. If people trust their instincts, they will most often do what is right. It's when they ignore what is right and try to cut corners that they get themselves into trouble. Tell your staff always to do what they think is right. Do what is right yourself. It is a powerful message.

❏ *Live the values.* You are under the microscope at all times. You can't fool people. How people see you behave is what they will believe. How they see you behave toward others will be how they anticipate you will behave toward them. Everything you do and every action you take is watched. Don't think you can substitute words for deeds. Vary from your course only once, and it will take you a long while to get your credibility back. Live the values.

❏ *The toughest road may be the best.* Don't succumb to the shortcuts that undermine values.

❏ *Err on the side of fairness.* It will be remembered.

EIGHT

No More Training Wheels

The courage to let go

At Home . . .

Stephen woke up that morning in October more determined than ever. For weeks now, he had been telling everybody that he was four years old and didn't want training wheels on his bike any longer. His chest puffed out, his chin pulled in, and his mouth tightened, he strode into the kitchen that Saturday. Before anyone could say anything—even "Good morning"—he announced: "I'm going to throw my training wheels in the garbage today."

That was the tradition in our family. Whenever the training wheels came off the two-wheeler, they were off for good. No changing one's mind. No unscrewing the nuts, removing the wheels, and later deciding to put them back on. Once off—off for good.

In our family, we make a big deal of this major step. We've turned removing a bike's training wheels into a ceremony.

So Dad and Stephen went together to the garage to locate the right-size wrench. They tried different ones until they found one that fit. Dad made the first few turns to loosen the nuts, then Stephen finished the job by unscrewing them all the way and removing the training wheel brackets from the bolts. When both had been lifted off, Stephen took them, one at a time, and with a proud flourish threw them into the trash can. Then, meticulously, he closed the lid.

Ceremony over and commitment made. Now on to the hard part.

Stephen rolled the bike to the street. He was smiling that big grin of his. No reason not to let the world know how proud he was that he had made it past the first hurdle.

But taking off the training wheels was *only* the first step and Stephen knew it. As much as he might will it to be so, he didn't in fact know how to ride without that extra set of wheels. Well, he knew how—in theory. But now he had to learn "on the job" so to speak: learn by simply doing it. To his father, that meant Stephen, like his older brothers and sisters before him, had to be given the chance to fall, to pick himself up, and to try again.

Dad held the bike, keeping it upright as Stephen climbed on. Then, grabbing the back of the seat, Dad gave the bike a gentle push. Stephen started to pedal. Still holding on, Dad ran with the bike.

Little did Stephen realize how hard it would be to pedal, hold the handlebars straight, keep looking forward, and—oh, yes—not fall down. "Hey, Daddy, I'm doing it," Stephen yelled joyously. He turned his head. The handlebars turned. The bike careened to the left but Dad held on and kept the bike from falling.

Stephen tried again. Dad held on. A few more times he turned his head—then he got the message. Keep looking straight. Your shoulders follow your head. Your arms follow your shoulders. And, when your arms turn, so do your hands and so does the front wheel.

Now came the question parents dread. *When do you let the bike—and your child—go?* When would Dad let Stephen go riding down the road all by himself? It wasn't as if Dad had never faced this decision before. But each child is different. Each child learns at a different pace. And each child has to reach his or her own level of self-confidence before being able to go it alone.

There's no right answer—or wrong answer. With Stephen, "going it alone" didn't happen that day. In fact, it didn't happen for a few more weekends, during each of which Stephen kept trying. It took time for Dad to feel that Stephen could handle it. Finally, after some more falls off the bike—and not just a few Band-Aids—Stephen was ready.

And so was Dad. Dad let go and Stephen went down the street by himself. Of course, Stephen did turn his head . . . a little . . . a few times. The bike swerved back and forth and *almost* tumbled over. But it didn't—and Stephen straightened out. Finally, when the front wheel hit a curb, Stephen and his training-wheel-less bike came to a stop.

From then on, there were no second thoughts. Stephen knew how to ride a bike. When he turned five a few months later, he was racing down the street on his bike, taking hairpin turns, and experimenting to see if he could ride with "no hands."

At the Office . . .
On the surface, it seems simple enough. Teach your children to ride a bike. Give them time to practice. And, when they have the hang of it, let go and off they race down the street.

But, as every parent knows, this "simple task" is filled with agony and doubt—knots in your stomach. Anxiety that your son or daughter will get hurt. What is simple enough in theory doesn't feel simple in reality.

The critical decision is *when to let go*. In business, it's also a difficult decision. Do you let one of your staff go by herself to that critical business meeting, make that important sales call, or fly solo at that crucial presentation?

There is a difference, of course. In business, you're not taking a chance on someone getting physically hurt. Rather, you're faced with the possibility of *hurting the company*. When you decide to let an employee "go it alone," the risk is: Will she make the correct business decision, represent the company properly, ink that important sales contract responsibly, or present the company's strategy persuasively? All of these—and many more—are very important business tasks. And it is the leader who has to decide if others are ready to handle them.

Bikes or business, there is an important lesson that comes from flying helicopters. In the Army, the guidelines for training a student pilot to fly solo are very simple: a fixed number of hours in the classroom and then some number of hours at the controls, flying the helicopter with the instructor pilot alongside, sitting in the left seat. It's completely up to the instructor pilot to assess when the student is ready to fly safely around the traffic pattern, taking off and landing three times by himself, with no one else in the aircraft. This is not a simple decision. In fact, each time, it could be a fatal decision.

Still, there comes a time with every student when the instructor pilot has to make that decision: The instructor lands, unbuckles his shoulder harness, steps out of the aircraft and gives a thumbs up, signaling the student to slowly turn the throttle, lift the collective, push the left pedal, hold the cyclic, hover to the takeoff pad—and go it alone. In truth, the instructor cannot ever know with certainty if his timing is right and the student is ready. He only knows the answer for sure *after* the student pilot has successfully made it around the traffic pattern—not once, not twice, but three times.

There is no absolute guide when it comes to judging another person's readiness. So the instructor simply has to trust his or her experience and intuition to make the right decision. Interestingly enough, the decision often depends more on the instructor's self-confidence than on confidence in the student. Because it is the instructor pilot's judgment that is critical—everything rests on that.

Not all business people have been instructor pilots. But it is much the same kind of judgment and some of those same instincts which must apply when as a leader you are faced with the decision to let an employee fly solo.

The real key is courage. Whether you are letting go of your child as he rides a bike for the first time, stepping out of the cockpit to let the student fly alone, or sending one of your staff to that all-important business meeting *alone*—what you need most is courage. The courage to trust your own judgment. That *is* what it takes.

Keep in Mind . . .

As you encourage your staff to do new things and to do them on their own, think about the following:

❑ *Have the courage to trust your own judgment.* There are no sure answers for just about anything important in life, and that definitely includes the point at which one of your staff is ready to handle some important assignments on his own. So, make a fair evaluation, have confidence in yourself and have the courage to trust your judgment. Then, let them go at it.

❑ *Push them off . . . and let them go.* Talented people will respond to the challenge. Give them more freedom and more responsibility. Nothing worthwhile is utterly risk-free, but give them a chance. Business decisions are most often not a life-or-death issue. Push them to do things on their own. If they fail, they will learn from it. If they succeed, they will learn too.

❑ *Delegate and provide the tools for them to do the job.* You can accomplish only so much by yourself. If you want to lead larger and larger organizations, you will have to accomplish some things yourself and many other things through others. For that to happen, you need to be confident enough to delegate, teach, and then turn over the *tools of the trade.*

❑ *Give responsibility—plus authority.* If you want your staff to grow, give them greater responsibilities and the authority they need to get the job done. Let go of the bicycle seat and let them ride by themselves. Get out of the cockpit and let them fly.

❑ *When they fall, encourage them to go at it again.* The task may be important but there won't be life-or-death consequences if they make a mistake. If you thought they were good enough to handle the assignment on their own, continue to trust your judgment. Let them brush themselves off and try again. Don't let them sense that you're discouraged. Spur them on.

❑ *But, if they just can't do it, no matter how hard they try and how much you encourage them, move on.* None of us is perfect. If in the end it's clear that he just can't handle the job, then both of you need to talk about it, acknowledge the facts as they are and move on. It's much better that way. Better for you, better for everyone.

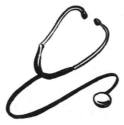

NINE

The Emergency Room

Keep your cool

At Home . . .

It was Thanksgiving. This was one of those great holidays. Every year, we all gathered together at the home of someone in the family for the Thanksgiving feast. This time, it was in Queens, New York. There were lots of kids, all over the house. Our six, plus at least a dozen more. Some of them were playing downstairs in Auntie's apartment. The others, upstairs in the one which belonged to Mom's younger sister, Sandy. You could hear the kids running around, up and down the stairs. And from the kitchen all those special Thanksgiving foods sent their delicious smells throughout the house.

It was Grandpa who used to cook the turkey and all the fixin's. Now, it was his daughters who did it. They cooked as a team, each making something. The sweet potatoes with marshmallows, the cranberry sauce, and the turkey—all of that turned out great. But the stuffing—that was a different matter. That they couldn't duplicate. It was Grandpa's triumph and only his. He made it with fresh chestnuts. Days of preparation went into it. And though many had tried, no one could make it quite like he did. There was something about the way he mixed the bread, the vegetables, the spices, and then those fresh chestnuts. Over time, it became clear that fresh chestnuts were only half of Grandpa's "secret ingredient." The other half—the half no one could duplicate exactly—was his unique way of blending *all* the ingredients . . . perfectly.

Now, the Macy's Thanksgiving Day Parade had come to an end. The Rockettes had danced at 34th street. The high school marching bands had passed by. The big balloon characters from the land of imagination had floated down the street with their handlers holding tight, fighting those sudden gusts of autumn wind. And now, all bundled up in gloves, a hat, and a red scarf—her smile warming up the cold morning—Katie Couric signed off for NBC, marking the end of another of the extravagant parades down the streets of New York City.

"Mom . . . Dad!" Sudden shrill yells coming from upstairs.

"Matthew's bleeding! He's got a cut in the back of his head!"

Our stomachs roiling, we both ran up the stairs, two steps at a time.

"Where is he?"

The other kids pointed. There was Matthew, lying on the floor. We'd find out what happened later—how a game of catch with his Aunt Sandy's dog Spunky had turned into an accident. We'd eventually learn all the details about how Matthew had fallen backward and hit the back of his head against an old, glass water bottle which had been lying on the floor filled with extra change. Right now we could see that he had cut his head on a sharp edge of shattered glass. The blood told us that much.

We knew we had to comfort him first and then look to see how bad it really was. Mom held Matthew in her arms, cradling his head, telling him that it would be okay. Dad could tell that the cut must be somewhere around the base of his skull but, with Matthew still agitated, we couldn't yet tell just where. It probably was only a matter of a minute or two, but it seemed like hours until Matthew settled down and we could see it.

It was pretty deep. And probably two inches long. Dad looked at Mom. Not too many words had to be spoken: *It would need stitches.*

"I need a clean towel," Dad said. "Let's get our jackets on. We need to take Matthew to the hospital."

Matthew was pretty quiet now. Matthew's Uncle Paul had said he would drive so that we would not have to spend time looking for a parking spot but could go right into the emergency room at Elmhurst Hospital. And Matthew's Uncle Claude had said he would call ahead to let the emergency room know we were coming.

With Matthew in our arms, we hurried into the emergency room. The nurse took one look at Matthew's head and brought us into one of the examining rooms so that a surgeon could take a closer look. We were lucky. We guessed that this must have been an unusually quiet Thanksgiving afternoon. The emergency room was relatively slow.

Matthew was still crying on and off, but he was pretty good for the moment. No hysterics. The pain had probably dulled even though it clearly was still there. The early healing of the cut had started, deep inside where the tissue starts to come back together.

The surgeon was a young woman. Probably in her early thirties. She wasn't a cosmetic surgeon but she had an aura of quiet competence. Besides, the cut was in a place where any scar would be covered by his hair.

Mom held Matthew close, his face nestled against her neck. That way the surgeon could examine him while Mom kept him quiet. The surgeon looked at the cut carefully and then went to work getting a small piece of glass out. She didn't say much. She just went about her business. She trimmed the hair near the cut and dabbed the area with iodine to sterilize it.

Mom kept Matthew quiet, talking to him about things they had done together and about what was waiting on the Thanksgiving dinner table. She kept him mentally occupied. She knew what Matthew liked: turkey, brussels sprouts, carrots, and salad. You see, Matthew—unlike our other children—absolutely loved vegetables. So it wasn't the apple pie and ice cream that would interest Matthew most. Rather, it was all those other things kids weren't supposed to like.

The surgeon turned to Mom. "We'll staple his head," she said. Nothing more. Just four words: "We'll staple his head."

Mom and Dad looked at each other. We'd already seen more than our fair share of stitches. But stapling? A first for us—the kind that elicits a dozen anxious questions . . . all at once. *Would the staples really go into his head? How did that work? Would they go right into the skull? Did it hurt? How do you get metal staples out? Would that hurt a second time, when they were pulled out?*

Poor Matthew. Poor Mom and Dad. But, we had a job to do: Our job was to make Matthew feel calm and secure. So when the nurse put the metal stapler against the back of Matthew's head and pulled the lever to let the staple go, neither of us let our apprehension show.

At the Office . . .

Every parent knows that home is the place where the unexpected happens.

No matter how hard we try, there will always be something that we didn't anticipate—something that we didn't know would happen.

Unfortunately, some of those events are traumatic. Some of them involve injury. Some of them involve disappointment. And many of them do get us upset.

In the case of little children and injury, what goes wrong can be very serious. It can be much more critical than a cut that needs stitches—or staples. There could be permanent injury or even a life-threatening situation. But that's life. That's life in the home.

And that's life at work. Difficult times cannot be avoided. There will be disappointments. There will be business strategies that don't work. And there will be financial targets that can't be met. They are just part of what happens.

In life, something will always go wrong. Unfortunately, we are not always in control of the situation. But the one thing we can control is how we deal with the situation. And that is key.

Mom and Dad are leaders of the household. How they respond to a tough situation will dictate how the household responds. They set the tone and the style.

In the same vein, the leader at work sets the tone and the style in the office and for the business. How the leader deals with pressure, how that person responds in a moment of crisis—how the leader keeps his or her "cool"—can make all the difference in the world. Especially when the going gets really tough.

Keep in Mind . . .

As you assume the responsibility of leadership in your organization, remember that you set the tone and the style. Your staff—the people you work with every day—will take their guidance from you. Keep the following in mind:

❏ *You are in the spotlight.* Don't forget that. All eyes are on you. How you behave will be how they behave. It's an enormous responsibility. And it is yours. If you have a crisis—if your plant explodes, if a worker gets sick or injured, if you are facing a financial crisis—think about how you should behave and then act that way.

❏ *Identify members of your staff whom you believe you can count on in a tough situation.* Imagine you are a pilot. Ask yourself, *Whom would I want in the seat next to me as I go into combat—whom can I count on to fly the aircraft if I can't?* Keep those people in mind. You may need to call on them.

❏ *You are the "buffer."* You're the leader. You get paid more because you're more experienced and better able to handle stress. Do it. Accept the pressure, deal with it and then put the problem in perspective so that your team can focus on how to solve it and get on with the job at hand. Keep in control. Identify the problem and let your team concentrate their energies on looking for solutions and moving beyond the problem, addressing other issues that require attention and action. If your team feels that you are not in control, they will lose confidence in the company's capacity to get beyond the crisis intact. And they will likely overreact. They may do too much, too little, take the wrong action—or take no action at all. If you, the leader, are not in control in a tough situation, the result could be devastating: a shaken company at best or, at worst, one poised to self-destruct.

❑ *Don't overreact and don't underreact.* Think the situation through. If you've never encountered a situation like this before, take a deep breath. Mentally work through a variety of scenarios. Ask for advice. And then, think again before you act. Do what is necessary—don't do more, but don't do less, either. If you keep your footing—your balance—no matter how rough the storm, your team will keep theirs. Your team will take its cue from how you behave. Never let them see you sweat. In a tough situation—in the middle of a crisis—you need to exude confidence. Sweat dripping from your brow doesn't help. In fact, it can cloud up other people's vision just when you need everyone to see things clearly. If a situation is indeed serious, tell them that. But tell them calmly. Their ability to handle the situation depends in great measure on your ability to assure them it can be done.

❏ *Focus on the goal you want, on the result you are seeking.* Don't get caught up in things that aren't critical. Keep your eyes fixed on what you need to do in order to move beyond the problem to the solution.

❏ *Assign tasks and ask for help.* Get others to share some of the tasks. That way you can concentrate on the key issues and get the problem solved as quickly as possible. Remember, you are the leader—but of a team.

TEN

Not Everyone Likes Vanilla

Let loose the entrepreneurial spirit

At Home . . .

The "ice cream man" came every evening during the summer. His white truck would round the corner carefully, usually around seven-thirty. He had the timing down perfectly—he knew just when to ring those bells. He knew lots of kids would be outside playing then. It was after supper but it wouldn't get dark for a while yet.

His name was Bob—easy to remember. He drove slowly toward the house, slowly enough so the kids could hear that circus tune as the truck approached. This was their cue to scream "The ice cream man's here!" and run to the front. Bob always smiled as he stopped the truck. He liked the kids. Plus he knew that, in front of our house, he'd make at least six sure-fire sales.

So many choices! All those pictures pasted on the side of the truck—so many different kinds of ice cream. Sandwiches! Cones! Ices! Push-up pops! So many temptations. You couldn't miss. Even the bold colors were delicious. The red and blue "firecracker" frozen popsicle. The green and yellow catcher's mitt with the pink bubble gum in the middle. Old-fashioned "creamsicles" and the traditional chocolate-covered "Good Humor" ice cream bar. And, of course, the ones with the most popular kids' characters emblazoned across the carton, licensed by the folks who bring us Nick Jr. and Saturday morning cartoons.

Bob was our kids' friend. Sometimes, he would lift the two youngest of them through the big window, right into the truck. They loved that and he knew it—to be close enough so they could *almost* touch all of the ice cream.

When Bob pulled up, six kids struggled for who could get to that window first. They had trouble taking turns. There was a little pushing and some shoving, but nothing mean, just mounting expectation of that first taste. No one wanted to run the risk of finding out that someone else had just gotten the last cotton candy swirl ice cream bar.

They wanted exactly what they wanted. And only rarely did any of the six choose vanilla. Sometimes

Nicholas would choose the same ice cream for a week straight. Matthew was as likely to decide on something different each day. Stephen would always choose the ice pop that had the brightest colors. Whatever, this had to be their choice. And theirs alone.

We liked the way Bob was patient with each child as all six took what seemed an eternity to decide what they wanted that day. He obviously understood that, for a little child, this was a major decision. If they didn't take the time to ponder—if they hurried their choice and selected the wrong one—that ice cream was likely to find its way into the trash. Or, worse yet, if it was one of the younger children, the mistake was just dropped on the ground after a single, disappointing taste.

At the Office . . .

We're all different. Distinct from one another. That's the way it is in childhood, and that's the way it is among adults. At work, as at home, it's vital to recognize those differences, respect them—and capitalize on them.

On the one hand, understanding and *using* the many differences and talents of your employees are key to entrepreneurial success. Because of that, our challenge as leaders is to find ways to let that spirit loose. Freed, it can make an employee's productivity soar—and a company's growth reach new heights. It can make the difference between keeping and losing your best people.

That means that leaders must give their staff the chance to develop—to learn what they don't like as well as what they do like. To experiment. To take risks. And, thereby, learn. Learn about themselves, about their strengths and about their weaknesses.

On the other hand, because each person is different, all need the chance to grow and stretch—in their own way. Providing opportunities for your employees to develop beyond their expectations—or yours—and even to discover new talents and abilities says volumes about the company and its values. A healthy dose of freedom builds extraordinary loyalty. And it helps to nurture a workforce that is truly first-class.

Great organizations, even those with limited resources, can have a meaningful impact on their employees' lives by creating new opportunities for them, because not everyone is best suited as a manager, as a secretary, or as an accountant. But they can only discover their true role by having the chance to try different jobs, learning about themselves as they go along, ultimately honing in on what they are *meant* to do.

When employees see that the culture in their company encourages them to test their limits, they will not only stay, but thrive. They will become genuinely entrepreneurial—creative and confident, recommending new approaches, new products, and new services.

And when the culture is "inclusive"—one in which they are part of the decision-making process and can have a voice—they can more fully participate and, thereby, learn and grow, often in ways they might not have expected.

If—by what you do and what you let them do—they feel that they can be entrepreneurial, they will have the courage to take risks. A courageous and confident workforce helps build a stronger company, one more able to adapt and innovate in order to meet the challenges ahead.

Keep in Mind . . .

It was a wise person who said: *You know why they make chocolate ice cream, don't you? Because not everyone likes vanilla!*

We all need a chance to grow. We all need a chance to stretch ourselves. We all need a chance to test our abilities.

The fact is that we thrive when we have the opportunity to develop in our own way, taking advantage of our unique talents and our differences.

Leaders want to keep their best people. And to do that, you need to give them new opportunities, new challenges, and you have to make them part of the team.

Think about how truly valuable your employees are to the company. Think about what you can do to keep your best people:

❏ *Encourage them to try something different.* Most people are willing to try something different—if they feel that it is okay to try. Those who will end up as your most productive staff members truly want to learn new skills and try tackling new assignments. Encourage that. It can mean the difference between a growing organization and one that teeters on the brink of failure.

❏ *Free the entrepreneurial spirit.* In a large organization, there is always plenty of room for the entrepreneur. But for the entrepreneurial spirit to thrive, staff members need to be able to make their own choices. Give them opportunities. Let them choose. When they make the selection, commitment goes with it and then ownership of the results, good or bad.

❏ *One of your jobs is to help them learn.* Invite them to try something new. Encourage them to take a risk. Then, let them go at it alone. Even when a lot is at stake, give people a chance to work out a solution on their own. By encouraging your staff to try something different, you help them learn about their strengths and weaknesses. They learn about what they like, what they don't like, what they are good at, and what they are not so good at. Help them discover themselves by challenging them with new assignments. You'll be surprised at how often your confidence will pay off.

❏ *Stretch.* Every so often, take a big leap and give a plateful of responsibility to someone you think

shows real promise, or even to someone who sur-
prises you by asking for it. To be realistic, sometimes
stretch targets don't work. But more often than not,
they do. Many people want just that kind of challenge. Select people well and then give them some
task which is more difficult than most. Most likely,
they will rise to the task and do more than even they
thought they could do. And when they have been
challenged, they grow and they are even more committed to the organization.

❏ *Create a dialogue and include them.* Ask your staff for
ideas about what they could do differently. When
they suggest an idea, consider it carefully. If it excites
them and it has a chance of helping you improve the
company, give them the freedom to go ahead and
run with it. Take a chance. If it works—and seems
to work well—let them help you identify what
should be done next.

❏ *Let them do it their way.* Accept the risk of them not
doing it your way. It could be that they're right and
you're wrong. Opening a dialogue means opening
yourself to new ideas and new ways of doing things.
That can be threatening, but it can also be very
healthy. What's more, the results can be startlingly
good. New ideas—with some risk taking—are vital
elements in an entrepreneurial organization and in
one that keeps its best people.

❏ *Encourage a frank and open discussion about their careers—what they should and can expect from the company and what you can and should expect of them.* Talk with your employees. Don't just evaluate performance. Ask them what they want to accomplish. Remind them that their careers are their responsibility—but you can help. Talk about career goals and aspirations. You can help them learn how to improve their work lives. But it must start with a sharing of views.

❏ *While you add "re-invention" to their agenda, add it to your own, too.* As you challenge your staff, challenge yourself to look at different choices. Think about how to reinvent yourself as well to keep the organization ahead of the pack.

❏ *Don't stand in their path.* When your employees are looking for new experiences and new opportunities, make sure you're not standing in their way. If you stand in their way, they will leave—maybe not right away, but pretty soon. Try to offer them real challenges. But if you can't come up with assignments that will stretch them, then help them find another company where they'll get those opportunities. In fact, encourage them to leave. Offer them leads and support in their search. There is no question that finding a replacement takes resources, time, and money. But you may actually be making an investment that pays off in two ways. First, you may hire exactly the right person for the job at hand. And, second, the employee who left may return in due course, with other useful experiences under his or her belt.

ELEVEN

When in Doubt, Sit It Out

If you're losing control, stop right there

At Home . . .

It was March 16, 1985. Winter hadn't yet turned to spring but the weather was starting to get warm. We were married late that Saturday morning at St. Bartholomew's in Queens, New York. The guests were mainly family, of course including Vera, Katrina, and Ted. So the Texas kids could be with us, we'd purposely set the date to fit in with their winter vacation. Since some of the family came from Connecticut, the reception was in Greenwich, an hour's drive from the church. But none of the guests seemed to mind. In our car, there were the five of us—with Mom in her wedding dress and Dad in his tux. It was quite a sight.

Early the next morning, car jam-packed, we set off for Vermont. Some might wonder at a five-person honeymoon. But we thought it just right to include the kids. That was the start of how we do just about everything: on the "family plan." This time, we would stay at a friend's house at the base of Stratton Mountain and spend most of the week taking advantage of the last of the winter snow.

The chatter at the kitchen table on Monday morning was all about the slopes. The snow looked pretty good, but was probably that typical New England cover the ski reporters like to call "packed powder and loose granular." We all knew that was code language for man-made snow pumped on top of what had frozen the night before when the temperature dropped. But we didn't mind. We knew we would have a good time. After all, it was our honeymoon. As for the kids, they were geared up to enjoy whatever snow there was, regardless if man or God "made" it.

Vera was a pretty good skier. She was fourteen then and had been skiing for quite some time. Katrina would be ten the following month and was getting more confident on skis all the time. Ted, not yet five, was just getting started. Still, true to form, he loved to go fast.

Renting skis at the base of the mountain always took time. The *lines*. The wait. Getting the bindings adjusted for each child. Finding the correct-size boots—not too

big, not too tight. Signing the forms. Giving over your
driver's license as a security deposit. And then lugging all
that equipment to the lodge to buckle the boots and get
the skis on right.

No question. We were going to the top of the mountain. We knew there were some beginner trails up there.
Mom and Dad had been skiing for many years but this
would give everyone a chance to warm up gradually and
then, as the kids got more confident, work our way
together to some more challenging slopes.

The two girls came off the lift first. They rounded
the bend and waited. Mom and Dad followed close
behind with Ted.

We started down the trail, the wind in our faces, the
hard snow crackling under the steel edges of the skis.
Mom was in front, with the kids spread out in the middle
and Dad trailing behind, keeping watch. This first run
was great. Not too steep. Just right for getting a little bit
of confidence. When we gathered at the bottom, everyone felt pretty good.

Up to the top again.

The dismount from the chair lift was pretty easy
because it was early in the day and there were no ruts to
catch the edge of anyone's skis. We looked around for
another trail to try.

"Let's take this one," said Vera. Katrina agreed. "This
one" was an intermediate trail. But we *were* warmed up.
All five of us gave a thumbs-up, and off we went. It wasn't

steep. But there were some turns and the trail got pretty narrow at times. The girls were in control. Crossing from side to side to keep their speed in check and stopping every once in a while to regroup. Mom was ahead of the pack again and Dad was following behind.

But Ted had a different idea. On the first run, he had been cautious, snowplowing his way down. By now, though, he had figured out that if he put his skis side by side he could pick up quite a bit of speed. That definitely was more fun. Besides, he liked the wind in his face—and the sensation of going fast—that he *loved.*

As Ted rounded one of the turns, he saw that the trail straightened out. In the flash of an eye, he was off and racing. Skis parallel. Leaning a little forward. He gained speed. He was only about three feet tall—pretty close to the ground—which made for very little wind resistance.

You could barely hear his skis on the snow. They were flat. No edges cutting any corners. Just skis running fast on the icy surface.

Seeing Ted come racing down toward her, Mom yelled, "Ted . . . stop!" But Ted was hurtling downward. Vera and Katrina yelled his name, but that didn't help. In fact, it only made things worse.

"I can't!" Ted screamed.

From about fifty feet away, Dad shouted, "Sit down, Ted. Just *sit down on the snow.* You'll stop."

But Ted had lost control. Completely. Things were going much too fast.

At that moment, the trail took a gradual turn to the left. Ted couldn't turn his skis soon enough. He hit the snow fence with his right side. It fell down and he rolled over twice, his skis flipping up in the air. He didn't cry. He just lay there, probably wondering how all that happened so fast.

Dad skied over to his side. Checked to make sure that he wasn't hurt. Reached down to help. Lifted him back onto his skis. And said only, "Remember what we talked about. *When in doubt, sit it out.*"

At the Office . . .

It's not only on the ski slope that you run the risk of losing control. It happens in business as well. But the same rule applies.

When in doubt, sit it out.

In business, you need to stop—really stop. Take a few deep breaths. Then make sure you have all the facts. Ask for input, advice. Turn to someone who has more experience. Then, having listened carefully, think the situation through once more. Be sure you're back in control. Now get going again.

There are plenty of business situations where you need to pause and rethink what is going on and how you are handling the situation.

If you're making an acquisition and the *chase* has become more important than thinking through how to make it *work*—you'd be better off if you stopped and reviewed the whole picture.

If you're developing what you think is an exciting new product, and market research is beginning to surface some troubling data—stop and rethink the situation before you go too far.

If you're angry at the way someone has behaved and your first impulse is to fire that employee on the spot—take a deep breath, maybe two or three, then calmly evaluate various ways you can deal with the situation.

The point is simple. When things are too emotional, when things get moving too fast, or when your eagerness to get something done could be clouding your view—*you must pause.* It doesn't mean you won't continue on the track you were going. It doesn't mean you would do anything very differently. It means you will stop for a moment—or as long as it takes—to make sure that you have all the information necessary to decide on the right course of action.

The last thing you want to do is go blindly down a path when all the warning signs are there and you're simply moving too fast to pay attention to them.

When a child is skiing too fast, it can be very dangerous. When an executive in a business situation is moving too fast into uncharted or unfamiliar territory, that too can have lasting consequences.

Keep in Mind . . .

Think about the following:

❑ *Stay in control.* Never let a business decision get to the stage where you feel you have lost control. Retain your command of the situation—and of yourself.

❑ *If you feel as though you are losing control, stop and "sit it out."* Take time out to reexamine what you are doing and to make sure you're on the right track.

❑ *If it doesn't feel right, it probably isn't right.* It has been said before, but it's worth saying again: *You must trust your gut.* If something doesn't feel right, stop. Take a step back and look carefully at what you are doing. Ask yourself if you think this really is the right course of action.

❑ *Reach out for help.* If you have doubts, ask for more information. And don't hesitate to ask others for their advice. They may have a useful perspective to share, perhaps one that could save you from making a serious mistake.

❑ *Learn from the past.* There's not a lot that's brand new. That means that someone else has probably encountered a situation similar to the one you're dealing with. Maybe you yourself have been in a situation not unlike this before. Think back. Are there parallels here? What did you learn? Act on it, now.

TWELVE

Grandpa's Way of Doing Things

Pride and passion: Not just good—very good

At Home . . .

Mom loved to bake. She learned it from her Dad. His name was Ernest and he was a great chef. He'd learned how to cook and bake in Switzerland where he was born. His older sister had her own restaurant. He'd gone to a first-rate culinary school, in a small town north of Lake Geneva. Then he'd worked onboard a ship in order to get passage to the United States in the late 1930s. He'd had the best training a young chef could ask for and, once in New York City, he worked at a five-star hotel. After that, he'd been the head chef in one of the best-known catering halls—receptions for five hundred guests were not unusual and huge parties to mark all sorts of occasions were commonplace.

Grandpa married Carmella, the brown-haired Dutch girl he met at a Swiss Club dance one summer's evening. A few years before the first of their five children was born, he and Grandma moved to Montreal. Straightaway, the Ritz Carlton hired him. On his day off, he and Grandma would sit out in the courtyard restaurant of the hotel and watch the ducklings waddle up and down the ramp which connected their little house and the pond.

But that was years ago. In good time, Grandma gave birth to Mom—the fourth of five children. By then, Grandma and Grandpa had returned to New York and lived in Queens.

A chef's hours are long and hard. So it was Grandma who watched over their five kids as they grew up. When Mom or any of Mom's three sisters were late getting home at night, you would always see Grandma leaning out of their second floor window, waiting to catch the first glimpse of Doreen, Linda, Sandy, or Mom coming up the street. If they were late—and, like all kids, of course they sometimes were—Grandma would let them know. With four girls growing up, she had to be protective. And when that meant laying down the rules and enforcing them, Grandma was on the job full time.

From the beginning, there was a special closeness between Mom and Grandpa. They sensed things the same way. It was almost as if their minds were in sync, so they never needed a lot of words to communicate.

Grandpa came home late most nights—only after he'd finished ordering all the ingredients for the next day's menu at the restaurant. Inevitably, he arrived home very tired. He'd worked in the kitchen for fourteen hours—with only a few short breaks between the meals. When, finally, he did get home, he never wanted anything to eat. By then, food was the last thing he wanted to think about.

Morning would come soon enough. And there would be Mom in the kitchen making Grandpa breakfast, a few hours before he had to return to the restaurant and start preparing the soups and sauces and baking the pastries for those who would come to dine that day.

Grandpa had taught Mom how to bake. He never *explained* how. Nothing was written down. Her challenge was to watch—and remember. He'd say, "Just take some sweet butter." And he'd put the knife into the butter. With a twist of the wrist, he'd cut off a portion and expect that she could follow his example on her own the next time. Mom would ask, "But how much?" He'd say, "*This* much." She'd simply have to pay closer attention and figure it out. And she did. Through all the years until he passed away, she watched him create his specialties, over and over again.

Grandpa was gentle. When he spoke, he never raised his voice. Cooking was his craft and he *honored* it. He cooked with nothing less than passion, tasting every step of the way. He was his own worst critic. If it passed his test—if he thought it was good—then it was good. That was that. If it didn't pass his test, then it wasn't good enough, no matter what anyone else said.

When he didn't think the cake was just right, he'd mutter to himself, criticize the coarseness of the flour, smell the butter and check the temperature of the oven to make sure it was accurate. At the restaurant, the younger chefs—those still trying to earn the right to wear the chef's hat—would say that he was from the "old school." They meant it as a criticism. He heard it as a compliment. He knew how things could be done when you took the time—because you cared. Because "just right" was the standard that had to be met. To him, cooking and baking wasn't a job. These were his passions and they came from somewhere deep inside. They were achievements he could be proud of. A life he took pride in living.

It was no surprise that Mom felt the same way. She'd learned that at his side, the same way she'd learned his techniques. He never talked about the prizes he won for his cooking or for one of his other passions—ice sculpting. But, when they lived upstairs in that two-family house in Queens, she had seen the plaques tucked away on the top shelf of his closet.

And, now, one day, quite unexpectedly, our oldest son Michael—who had never met his Mom's Dad—went over to the stove and said, "Mom . . . will you teach me to bake those cakes you make?"

Apparently, for some time, he'd been quietly watching his Mom. Now, something already passed down from one generation to the next came to the surface in the third generation.

"Sure—if you really want to learn," Mom replied. She had a few doubts, though—not about the genuineness of his desire, but about how best to teach him what she knew. Her Dad had had a hard time explaining to her how he made those cakes. Maybe she would, too. They'd have to see.

"Can we make one today?" Michael asked.

You know how it is with kids. If they have an idea, they don't want to have to wait to move on it. And, if you don't understand that, well—they think—you'll never really understand anyway. So there's no use trying to discuss whether it would be better to bake the cake today or wait until tomorrow.

"Okay," Mom said. "Let's see if we've got everything. While I look for the vanilla, Michael, you go downstairs and bring up one of those blue and white, five-pound bags of flour."

No argument there. He was back in a few minutes, carrying the flour with both hands to make sure the bag wouldn't drop. What a mess that would be. He knew who would have to sweep it up. And—that would be that for the cake. No flour, no cake. Simple. Even worse than cleaning up, the real mess would be having to wait to embark on this latest adventure of his.

Michael saw to it that the bag didn't fall. Because he was on his way to learning what Grandpa had passed on to his Mom.

At the Office . . .

Whether it's in the kitchen or in the office, there is no substitute for pride and passion. No substitute for getting it right.

In fact, pride and passion are critical ingredients in successful organizations. Mind you, neither implies arrogance. Rather, they're about its opposite—humility.

In a thriving organization, pride and passion lead to sharing knowledge. They lead to a culture where people learn from others by watching and listening. To a culture where traditions that foster excellence and knowledge are *honored.*

Pride and passion are motives for doing the very best you can. For not accepting second-rate performance from yourself or others. And never settling for a job half done.

Pride and passion mean building a company or organizational history where values are nurtured so they can be passed on undiminished from year to year and generation to generation.

Pride and passion inspire the desire to learn—to learn from others when you recognize that what they have to offer will add to your fund of knowledge and skills.

Your organization's goal should never be less than excellence. And a parallel goal should be to make sure that your organization's level of skill continues to thrive, long after any particular individual has retired or left for another job or another city.

Pride and passion mean being able to get out of your own skin long enough to accept the fact that some people simply can't explain why they do what they do. What they do is intuitive. Believe them, and accept it.

The story goes that, when Michelangelo was asked how he was able to sculpt such extraordinary figures in marble, his answer was that he simply chiseled away at the marble until the figure emerged.

Writers can't always explain why they select one word over another. Painters can't say why they choose one color or brush stroke over another. Bakers can't explain how much sugar goes into the cake. Chefs can't explain how many grains of salt to use. And leaders can't always articulate why they make one decision over another.

But that's okay. Indeed, that's the way it should be. Often, intuitive choices are what distinguish the best from the rest.

Interestingly enough, it is pride and passion which give us the grace to accept that excellence can sometimes only be studied in *silence*.

Keep in Mind . . .

As you think about how to nurture passion and install a culture of pride in your company, keep the following in mind:

❑ *Be passionate—hire people who are passionate about their work.* Passion is a powerful force. People feel it. They respond to it. And they instinctively know its strength to create extraordinary success.

❑ *Encourage people to be proud of great work.* Pride, too, should be part of your organization's culture. People who feel good about what they do—who try always to do their best—are indispensable. They stand out from the crowd. Always. And they create success.

❑ *Celebrate "heroes."* In any organization, there are numerous people who live the values, the sense of pride, the passion—who work until the job is done right. These people should be held up as examples for others. They should be celebrated. They *embody* the values. And some of these heroes are the people who don't attract attention, but quietly go about doing their job.

❑ *Enrich your staff's sense of history.* Your organization's history is its heritage. Teach respect for the values and the cumulative accomplishments that have made it what it is today. Talk about some of the people who made a difference. Create a video—a living record—of the company. Ask founders and friends of the company to talk about what your company stands for and how it has behaved over the years. Update that video regularly so it continues to be relevant.

❏ *Be humble—don't be afraid to learn from others.* To reinvent the wheel is a waste of time and a waste of precious resources. Encourage your staff to learn from whatever source they can, especially from others who have made the company great—or who have made other companies great. Be humble enough to recognize that sometimes others just might have a better answer than you do. You do not know everything and you never will. So listen intently. Watch others. Learn. And grow.

❏ *Push yourself much harder than others would push you.* Be your own best friend and worst critic. Give yourself credit when you deserve it. But be equally candid about failures. Your staff should know that you will push yourself harder than anyone else would dare to. Because you know—deep inside—that *whatever needs doing needs to be done right.*

THIRTEEN

Doing Homework

Strengthen your human capital

At Home . . .

No one ever said it would always be easy.

The kids leapt off the school bus, ran down the street, and through the front door. You could hear the thud as they dropped their backpacks on the floor. On the run, they hardly paused to say ""Hi." The school day was over, and their thoughts were elsewhere as they climbed on to the kitchen counter stools looking for something to eat. They were all "starving," desperate for a snack and, of course, something to drink.

They *had* all worked hard that day. They got on the bus at 8:00 in the morning and returned well after 3:00 in the afternoon. That was almost seven hours in school. Of course, there were breaks for recess, gym, lunch, and even some free time. But for almost any student, especially an elementary school child, the school day is long. There's a lot to learn. That calls for a lot of concentration. And it doesn't stop, not even when school is over for the day.

Michael, at eleven the oldest, finished his sandwich and, without missing a beat, pulled up a chair to the long kitchen table. He took a schoolbook from his backpack, slipped out his homework assignment, and set to work. The answers to the division problems came pretty easily. The spelling assignment, too. The multiple choice geography questions were a snap.

James took small bites of his snack. He turned the channel to Nickelodeon. He always needs a little more time to wind down. He's the kind of child who will do everything he's supposed to, but in his own time. Same as yesterday and the day before, though, it's not too long before he hears his name called. "James, finish up and get started on your homework." Today, as usual, he's quick to reply, "Oh, why now? I'll do it later." And he will.

Angelica's very eager to get her homework done. She wants to get it over with so that she can get outside and spend some time playing with her friends. Every day, they talk about getting together after school.

Math is the challenge for Angelica, especially word problems. You know, the ones that start out hard and get even tougher when they involve fractions, decimals and some complex math concepts: "Two trains leave different stations one hour apart. . . ." But Angelica is a hard worker and, with a little bit of coaching, she reasons her way through each problem. When she comes across a particularly difficult question, she'll stop, come close by and gently ask for just the little help she needs. She gets the assignment done without complaint—earning her that playtime she wanted. Because she did what she had to do first.

Our three oldest are very different from one another. Only a year apart in age, each learns differently from the other two. Pace and ease are different. One works more independently than the other. One finds the work easy, another finds it challenging. But, in the end, each one does the work before playtime begins.

They have to. That's the rule in our house. It was a decision we made when Michael, our oldest, began first grade. All the children have to get their homework done before they go out to play.

And we don't do their homework for them. We're there to help, but they have to do it. That's the only way they will learn.

As in all homes with young children, morning rolls around pretty quickly. And the children who did their homework when their minds were still in gear will be best prepared for the coming day.

There are probably few efforts more frustrating than trying to get your children to do homework. Why? Because they don't see its importance. They simply don't see it. For them, homework is just a chore—like picking up their room. But you recognize how important it is for them. It reinforces learning. They start to reason on their own. And what is really extraordinary is they begin to *think*. They begin to think about how one particular homework problem actually relates to other things they do. The process isn't linear and it doesn't make for an overnight change. But it happens. And it goes on happening. Doing homework equips your children to make mental leaps that stimulate creativity. They are learning that they can develop ideas, even come up with brandnew ones.

You can't go through that process for them. At times, it may actually seem easier to do some of their math problems, or just plain tell them what the answer is to a history question. And it is easier—but only in the short run. And the most destructive thing about the short run is its brevity. Short-term solutions do not make things better in the long run. In the long run, what works is *work*.

If you do it for your children, they'll never be able to do it for themselves.

At the Office . . .

In a very competitive business environment, innovation is the price of survival. And "homework" is a means to get there. In fact, it is the responsibility of the leader to create a culture in the organization where "homework" is valued—that's one of his or her ongoing "homework" assignments.

Leaders—the ultimate mentors—need to point employees in the right direction. Employees need to be challenged and encouraged to do their own "homework."

This can mean suggesting that a staff member talk with a colleague to get some guidance. It may mean pointing out that not everything that needs to get done can or will always get done during the workday. So it can mean suggesting staying late or coming in on Saturday or Sunday to get a particular job done. It can mean recommending one of the training courses your organization gives so that he or she can develop the necessary skill to do the job at hand. It can mean offering to send that promising employee—that rising young talent—to a seminar, to graduate school, or to an executive training course.

Homework also means taking the extra time and thought to reason through a challenge, consider the pros and cons of alternatives, and come up with what is the dazzlingly right solution. Some of these solutions may seem to be "off the wall." But, throughout history, some of our greatest inventions and innovations appeared, at first glance, to be crazy ideas. They were often the result of approaching the same challenge from not one, but two or three or four angles, because the right answer may lay hidden behind a more obvious one.

It can be hard work. But it *is* necessary! Encouraging employees to think things through more than once, do enough research, look at a particular assignment from a new vantage point, and then come up with a range of new and different solutions, can mean the difference between the ordinary and the extraordinary. *The breakthrough*—that's what "homework" can accomplish.

To excel, people will have to study on their own, learn from others and get additional training—sometimes after work. They'll have to explore "new idea territory," even when the terrain is rough.

Another thought: If you cut up their work in bite-size pieces and feed it to them that way, they'll never learn how to chew a problem down to size on their own.

Homework ensures that we and our employees are prepared. Prepared for the new challenge, prepared to broaden our vision, prepared to conjure up a truly daring new idea. Prepared to think differently than we've ever thought before.

Keep in Mind . . .
The last thing any of us needs is mediocrity. In anything. At any time. We don't want it for—or from—our chil-

dren. And we certainly don't want it at work. The fact is, if we want to have a successful and thriving organization, we can't tolerate mediocrity in our product or in our staff.

Homework vaccinates against mediocrity. It elicits excellence.

It strengthens your human capital. It places the organization in a stronger position to deal with new challenges. It also prepares us to take advantage of unanticipated opportunities—which some might call luck or chance—which we otherwise might miss.

To create a working environment which encourages your employees to do their homework—make sure they're prepared, take the time, and make the effort to do their own thinking each and every day—you should consider the following:

❑ *Remember, among the most valuable assets in your company is your human capital.* As every business school teaches, in addition to a company's tangible assets, there are intangible assets. And, among those, human capital—your people, their skills and talents—is key. A dynamic, *learning* organization continually strengthens that asset. That requires hard work, focus and "homework." And it creates success.

❑ *Set your company's standards very high.* Encourage aspirations. Let everyone know that you will accept only the best. Given the pace of business, sometimes you might be tempted to relax this standard of excellence. Don't. The idea is to create a corporate culture that looks for results which exceed expectations.

❑ *Behave like Socrates.* Question, question, and question some more. Force your employees to explain what they think and what they recommend. Don't let them get by with obvious solutions. Press them. At every turn, ask *Why?*

❑ *All the while, never forget that each employee is different.* Each person is unique—both children and adults. They learn at different speeds. They are motivated in separate ways. And they have strengths that vary dramatically. But for just those very reasons, each one of them has the potential to make a great contribution to the organization—in a different way.

❑ *Push the limits of self-expectations.* Give your employees assignments which push them beyond what you *know* they can do. Push them to push themselves by asking them to accomplish something difficult—beyond their apparent limits. They will grow with the challenge and will value the confidence you have put in them. And they will work hard—often on their own, after hours, and on weekends—in order to live up to your confidence.

❑ *Assign "work homework."* Don't hesitate to ask your employees to take on special assignments. To research a new development by a competitor. To examine how another company does some of the same things you do. To look into innovative ideas developed by a business completely unrelated to yours and explore whether the way they do things applies to your business. By doing this, you will encourage your staff to look for breakthrough solutions in offbeat or otherwise unexpected places.

❏ *Demand nothing less than "completed staff work."* In the military, completed staff work means that something is ready for signature. In business, completed staff work means that it is the very best it can be. When your employees think they've done enough—and it isn't 100 percent complete—get them to try one more time.

❏ *Make clear that each employee is in charge of his or her own career.* And doing one's homework is "Step One" on that career path. As much as we may want to help and guide others in their careers—just like doing homework for your children—it doesn't work in the long run. Make sure that every staff member knows that, if he or she wants to grow and advance, there's only one person who can make it happen.

❏ *Provide the tools to grow by.* Core skills training, advanced training programs, and education assistance plans are very important instruments for an organization that really believes in excellence. Having these kinds of programs in place communicates a company's values very strongly. And helps put mediocrity in its place—*out*.

FOURTEEN

I'm Sorry, Ms. Gioieni

*Acknowledge mistakes, accept responsibility,
and move forward*

At Home . . .

It started out like any other day of the week. Six lunch bags were assembled the night before. Two bologna sandwiches, one with a little bit of mayonnaise and the other with none—not even a drop. One turkey sandwich with lettuce. Two peanut butter and jelly sandwiches with the crust cut off. And one peanut butter sandwich—no jelly. Six juices. Six cookies for the afternoon snack. And napkins, of course.

That morning, four took showers. The others had done so the night before. Then breakfast for everyone:

mostly cereal. Some Cheerios. Others wanted Frosted Mini Wheats and some even Froot Loops. Three had orange juice as well.

Among them, they had to tie twelve shoelaces. Brush more than 150 teeth. Comb their hair. And finally sling six backpacks over twelve shoulders as they walked out the front door and down the street toward the place where the school bus would come to a stop.

There was nothing unusual about today. It was like so many others. The kids seemed in good spirits. Michael ran ahead toward the bus stop, James quickly following. Angelica wasn't far behind. And Nicholas, on his way to finishing up first grade, stopped to pick up a soft baseball that had been left in the street overnight.

It was just about noon when Mom got the call from the school. When you hear the school secretary on the phone, you can't help it—your stomach tightens and your mind goes in different directions. Your child fell in the playground. Or your child is running a high fever and the school nurse needs you to come by and take him home.

Fortunately, none of that was the case today.

No. Nicholas was being punished. He had "lunch detention."

Nicholas? Can you believe it? Of all the kids, Nicholas never seemed to do anything wrong. And now—he's got "lunch detention."

Ms. Gioieni, Nicholas's first grade teacher, got on the phone. Nicholas, she said, had been stomping around.

Not in the middle of the classroom, she went on. He'd been stomping around in the large garbage can she kept by the wall for all those discarded papers and the lunch leftovers. Well, we all know that kids fool around, so that didn't seem to warrant detention.

There was more.

He'd also been a *wise guy*. Ms. Gioieni had asked, "Nicholas, Why are you doing that . . . stomping around in the garbage can?"

Without any hesitation—and in a matter-of-fact way—Nicholas stepped out of the garbage can, stood straight up and said in an unwavering voice, "Because— it's a free country."

Well that did it. Even though Ms. Gioieni could hardly contain her laughter—let alone her smile—as she listened to that answer, she knew she had to do some-thing—so she told Mom. What would the other kids think? How would they behave?

So lunch detention it was for Nicholas. He wouldn't be able to spend his lunch hour playing and running with the other kids outside. No—he'd have to spend it inside, sitting quietly, with just his teacher in the classroom.

Yuck.

Not a place any seven year-old would want to spend time. It wasn't jail, but Nicholas must have found it a close second. Certainly, it wasn't pleasant for him. But it also wasn't enough. Ms. Gioieni knew that Nicholas had to acknowledge that what he said was disrespectful. With that in mind, Ms. Gioieni told him that he would also have to write a letter home, explaining how he behaved that day.

He carried the letter home that day after school—it lay crunched up on the very bottom of his backpack. He hoped against hope that Mom wouldn't say anything. But Mom wasn't about to ignore the call she'd received. After all, how else would Nicholas learn that he had to take responsibility for his actions?

Then she read the letter:

Dear Mom and Dad

Today I got lunch detention and I was fooling around in music and I said to Ms. Gioieni that it is a free country. When she said to not step in the garbige can. I will not fool around.

Love Nicholas

Mom also had a hard time hiding her smile. It really wasn't such a big deal. But then again it just might be.

"When Dad comes home," Mom said, "we'll have to decide what to do about this, Nicholas."

The decision actually was pretty clear.

Shortly after dinner, we told Nicholas to sit down at the kitchen table. He knew he would have to write the letter he would give his teacher the next morning. He wrote:

Dear Ms. Gioieni

I was fooling around and today was
disrespectful to you. I'll be better and try not
to do that again. I promiss and I'm sorry.

Love Nicholas

At the Office . . .

There's no question that when you're looking at a child
who has taken a misstep that's more endearing than
enduring, there's a humorous aspect to the incident.
Besides, everyone makes mistakes. Children *and* adults.
We all do. Often. That's only human.

But if mistakes go ignored, they often lead to bigger,
more serious mistakes. So for children, parents, and business leaders alike, the critical issue is to acknowledge the
mistake. Learn from it. Don't try to blame others. Try not
to make the same mistake again. And move on.

While growth and financial success for a company
clearly mean moving forward, reaching those goals also
means that you have to take the time to look objectively
at the past and learn from it. There's no reason to make
the same mistake twice.

Interestingly enough, Nicholas's comment about a
free country had much more meaning than he could, at his
age, imagine. The simple fact is that it is only in a free
country where you can have both the responsibility for

leading a business and the freedom—the authority—to do what you think best.

As a leader, it is your responsibility to build a culture where people acknowledge their mistakes, don't dwell on them, and move ahead.

This is a skill that can be learned. For many, it can be very difficult to learn. When it comes to parenting, frankly it's often a lot easier to shrug an incident off as a harmless prank than to deal with it. However, while "shrugging" may work in the short run, and perhaps avoid some conflict and even pain, it sure doesn't work in the long run. It's not the right thing to do when you are bringing up children. And it shows equally bad judgment when you are running a business or any other kind of organization. In fact, shrugging off a mistake can in itself be a very serious mistake.

Keep in Mind . . .

As a leader, one of your objectives should be to create a culture of results. To make that happen, think about the following:

❑ *Accept responsibility and be straightforward.* None of us are perfect. In fact, we will never be. But take a candid look and move ahead.

❑ *Remember, no one likes doing business with people who make excuses and can't accept responsibility.* The fact is that you will lose customers, clients, and employees if you don't accept responsibility. No one wants to listen to someone spout excuses. Respect will be quickly lost. And, within your own organization, avoiding responsibility for a mistake will undermine your credibility.

❏ *Stand up straight and acknowledge what went wrong, then move on.* Admit your mistake. Do not try to explain it away. But neither should you go on beating yourself up—either publicly or privately. Self-recrimination that goes on beyond straightforward acknowledgment of your mistakes is unnecessary and even unhealthy. You're as human as the rest of us. The right thing to do is to turn your focus to solving the problem. Remember, one of the keys to attaining—and sustaining—success is to keep your focus and not permit yourself to get distracted when things go wrong. Make it right!

❏ *Don't spend your time placing blame—build a culture of honest evaluation and results.* The fact is, blaming doesn't undo mistakes—or create success. Sometimes, it doesn't even make a difference. But analyzing what went wrong can be very helpful. We learn from it. We grow. Your staff will follow your example and learn to look objectively at performance. That process helps create a culture of honest evaluation: Honest and fair evaluation from the top down also strengthens the foundation of a learning organization.

FIFTEEN

The Excitement of Broadway

Why the arts belong in the workplace

At Home . . .

It was one of those iffy winter afternoons. The morning weather report said that some snow might be possible. Now, the sky to the west actually looked a little dark, so maybe this time the weatherman would be right. There wouldn't be any construction on Sunday, so the only thing standing in the way of getting to the city—and the theater—on time would be traffic. And that "maybe" snowfall.

The matinee started at two. Truthfully, it was a little daunting to think about taking all the kids. *What were the odds that six children would sit still for almost three hours? Would one or more wish they hadn't come and keep asking when it would be over? Would Matthew or Stephen team up to kick the seats in front of them, making two unfortunate theatergoers more and more irritated? How often would we have to tell them to "Settle down!" before they did? Or, just maybe, would the imagination of all six be captured by the actors on stage, the music, the songs, the scenery changes— the excitement of seeing a play unfold before their eyes?*

The tickets had been bought months earlier. It wasn't easy getting eight seats together for a popular Broadway show. Especially as those eight seats mustn't be too far back, or else the little ones wouldn't be able to see the stage and experience fully what was happening up there.

Now the day was here. There was time for a quick lunch before setting out. Something—enough we hoped—to tide them over until after the performance. Each of the five boys put on a jacket and tie, and Angelica wore a dress for this special occasion.

We left at about 12:30. That would be time enough to find parking close to the theater and to make it into our seats before the curtain went up.

A hush overtook the theater as the lights slowly dimmed. All six children were settled in their seats. Some sat back—the big kids—and the others sat on the front edge of their seat cushion to get a better look. Not a sound was heard from any of them as the orchestra began to play and the music spread gracefully throughout the theater. The curtain slowly rose from the stage floor to the proscenium arch.

It was *The Sound of Music.* Literally and figuratively. And as a distant glimpse of the Austrian Alps started to take shape in the background of the stage, the hills, indeed, *were alive with the sound of music* for these six little people. Still not a sound from any of them, their customary activity stilled by awe. We ourselves were quieted by how engulfed they were by what was happening on stage. Their eyes darted back and forth as they watched, listened, and let their imagination take in all that was happening in front of their eyes.

Maria, her wild spirit struggling at times with the rigors—and pull—of the convent. The emotional struggle within Captain Von Trapp. The power of music to revive joy in the seven Von Trapp children. Love found when it was least expected. And the serenity that comes with standing up to oppression.

We didn't expect all those messages to register with our children as they watched the story unfold. And they probably wouldn't be thinking about faith and personal conviction at high cost or unanticipated joy during a painful time either on the journey home or when they lay in their beds that evening. But important messages have a lasting shelf life in the mind—and heart—and would, we felt, be there for our children to consider at a later day, enriching their lives in ways we would not presume to foretell.

Right now, in the theater that winter afternoon, all six seemed to be transported to a different world on the magic carpet of beautiful music. Gift enough for now—for them and for us.

At the Office . . .

Whatever your organization—whether it's for-profit or nonprofit, education or government, whether it's a business which centers around consumer products, technology, services or industrial manufacturing—you can't be a successful leader if you don't have focus and if you're not absolutely dedicated. You do need to be driven. Of that there is no doubt.

But you also need something else. You need perspective—a broader view of life. You need a window on creativity and on imagination. You can get some of that from work. But you also need the arts: books, music, theater, painting, film, sculpture.

Because all these are part of the totality of life, they can enrich your work—and they *will* enrich your life.

In theory, a business leader doesn't need to attend the theater, the opera, or museums. At first glance, the arts may not seem to have a lot to do with strong financial performance or leading the charts in market share. But, in reality, to be successful you have to be a person of breadth. With breadth comes balance. And context. And the arts help bring those into your life.

The arts can also make you a wiser leader. The insights they give you can add a new dimension to your dealings with people, broaden your perspective as you relate to customers, clients and business associates. One of the most powerful lessons in life is the extent to which the arts can enrich one's capacity to make the right kinds of business decisions.

In addition, the arts create opportunities for you to reach out in different ways to your employees. In business, especially when there too often need to be very long hours, weekend work, vacations delayed, and other personal sacrifices made in order to compete successfully, it's easy for people to miss the chance to go to the theater, visit a museum, or spend a day at the zoo.

Those opportunities are important in their lives as well.

Keep in Mind . . .
The arts do enrich our lives—in so many ways. Consider what they—and you—can do:

❏ *Have balance in your own life.* Each of us—regardless of our position or our line of work—needs to have a life outside of work. It makes us stronger. It makes our lives fuller. And when others know there's balance in our life, they are more likely to accept that the decisions we make are the right ones. Then they can believe in us as a human being, as a person who's more than just the boss.

❏ *Think of the theater or the arts when you want to reward your staff for doing an especially good job.* When people have done a great job, thank them, and invite them to take their husband, wife, or partner, go to the theater and have a quiet dinner together. They may think of it only as a reward—and it is a reward. But for the company, it's also an investment—an investment in developing greater fullness in the lives of your employees, and multiplying their chances of becoming even more productive members of your team. If they are more successful, the organization will be, too.

❏ *Bring the theater or music to the office.* If you have a cafeteria, a public space, a lobby, or a large conference room, bring in a quartet to perform or an author to give a reading for your staff. You could do it during lunch, you could do it late in the day, or you could use the office space on weekends.

❏ *Create an outreach program with a local school, historical society, or music group.* You don't always have to give money in order to provide support for a worthwhile organization. You can provide "in-kind" services. For example, work with a local school to help their young writers by printing a collection of their short stories in booklet form which the school can then sell to raise funds. Or give people time off to work in neighborhood projects, painting, cleaning, or helping with the elderly. Or provide services—accounting, construction, consulting—to local non-profit organizations.

❏ *Find a way to use the arts and culture to bring creativity to the workplace.* Invite people from the theater and the art world to participate in wide-open brainstorming and creative sessions. Ask some of them to give you their views on product design or customer service. You will undoubtedly enrich your office environment by reaching out to those in different worlds and from different occupations. No question about it: They will stimulate innovative thinking and encourage creativity.

❏ *Exhibit the talents of your own people.* Many of them—employees at all levels inside the organization—paint, draw, sculpt, or have other artistic talents and interests. Support them. Encourage them. Create an informal exhibit or gallery in the office or at the plant to display the creativity of those who work for you.

❏ *Look at your organization's corporate giving programs to see if there are ways you could target that money to bring the visual arts, music, or theater into the lives of those who work for you.* There is nothing wrong with using corporate philanthropic resources to enrich the lives of those who work in your company. In fact, that is a very appropriate goal for corporate giving. So look carefully at your own funding programs to see if some can be channeled to help broaden the lives of your own people.

❏ *Encourage your staff to spend some time helping out in schools.* Give them an afternoon or a morning off so they can help out at a local school or at the school their children attend. Or give them time off to teach in a class somewhere—inspiring future participation in your field. Encouraging the future of school children is time well invested, and the time spent could be a key factor in nurturing your employees' own respect for their career choice. There's no doubt the learning would go in both directions. It was a wise person indeed who once said: *The teacher learns more than the students.*

❏ *Encourage your staff to bring their children to the office from time to time—and you should bring your kids to the office.* Like the arts, the energy and fresh perspective of young people triggers in us a renewed openness to new thoughts, bright ideas, and a fresh viewpoint.

SIXTEEN

It's a Deal . . . Agreed?

Goal setting

At Home . . .

The time had come. The fact was, we had talked quite a lot about it with the three oldest kids. There had been issues we'd discussed more than once—or twice. Big ones, such as interfering with schoolwork, where they could go, and where they couldn't. There had been the very large issue of safety and not talking to strangers. We had tried to cover just about every topic, but there would inevitably be some we missed.

Because we already had one Internet provider, Michael, James, and Angelica all knew how to look for certain Web sites, the kinds for kids. At the same time, they knew they were to stay out of chat rooms. Still, the three of them had been campaigning for America Online (AOL) for weeks, and weeks. Why? Because all their friends "talked" together on line as "Buddies" every evening, comparing homework, just saying "Hi," telling stories about baseball practice, or planning the next chance to get together. These were, you understand, *major* reasons from their perspective.

There's no question, we had our concerns. *Would their schoolwork be affected? And what would happen to the time they're supposed to spend each night reading? How would we control what they did and where they went on the Web? Would the temptations become too much for them? Would it become too much for us? Would it work out all right for them—and for us?*

They did seem to understand that they were asking us to overcome some serious reservations. And they knew that, quite simply, we wouldn't let them subscribe to AOL without some clear understandings.

Kids need to know what they can and cannot do. And they need to know the consequences of their behavior: Discipline governs what they do, how they do it, and whether or not they are rewarded.

When it came to AOL, our kids also knew that they would have to help pay for it themselves. That's why they had two jars for their allowance: One was marked "Savings" so that they could buy some special things for themselves. Sometimes, they used that money for a new video game or some baseball cards. Other times, they used "Savings" money to help pay for a pair of very expensive sneakers. The other jar was marked "College." This wasn't for spending now—not for anything. This money went into the bank every two months, put away for their education. There wasn't any discussion about it. From the beginning, we made it clear to them that they would go to college and that they would help make it possible.

To get AOL, they would have to go into "Savings." We knew that would make them take this step much more seriously. They didn't protest, they must have instinctively understood why *this* wasn't going on Mom and Dad's tab.

Each of the three oldest kids unscrewed the top to their "Savings" jar. It was quiet at first. Sitting at the kitchen table, they carefully took out the dollar bills, along with some change. Michael had a pencil and paper, just in case. They slowly counted out their money.

The first step finished, Angelica called out: "How much do you have?" "What about you?" asked Michael.

James smiled. His whole face lit up. He was quick with numbers and he'd already calculated that they did have enough among them.

Carefully, they put their AOL fund in an envelope.

Phase One, accomplished. You could see in their eyes that what they were visualizing now was what it would be like sitting next to Dad when he logged on and got set up early the next morning.

That night, there wasn't much sleep for them. Tomorrow, Saturday, they would be online, ready to create their "buddy" lists. After lights out, we let the whispering go on much longer than we usually do. We took turns guessing what they were thinking—and what they were sharing so excitedly with each other. *Surely, friends' names for their "buddy" list. Did they already know those friends' screen names? And what screen name would they choose for themselves? What password? They already knew passwords had to have anywhere from three to ten characters—they'd proudly informed us of this piece of important information. But did they know what a character was? Could they, for example, use numbers and letters or just letters? We knew that Michael would be very protective of his password. James wouldn't be. And Angelica would probably tell her friends—but only her two best.*

We overheard them wondering aloud that night. Just how late will we be able to stay up to chat with our buddies? What time will Mom and Dad tell us that the computers have to be turned off?

Morning came very early. The older kids were at our bedside before the sun was completely up. That turned out to be a good move, because we got online without any delay, and when we had to talk to somebody at AOL, the phone was picked up almost immediately. How those kids' smiles grew as we went through the AOL setup and then downloaded 4.0. It was a proud moment for us, too. After all, the children had resisted many tempting things at toy and sporting goods stores to achieve their goal of getting AOL. And now, with the download almost complete, they each eagerly wanted to know, "Can I get on first?"

Not yet. We'd now reached Phase Two.

"No, not yet," Mom said. "First, we have to agree on the rules. Let's talk about them. Then, we'll write them down and each one of you can sign them. We'll tape that paper to the side of each computer and that way you won't forget," Mom said.

"Each one of you has to say what you think you can and cannot do once you're online," she told them. "Who wants to go first?"

This time, there wasn't a clamoring to be first. But, before long, they each came up with rules. "Turn off the computer whenever Mom or Dad say." "Take turns." "Be fair." "Be careful with the computer." "Only chat with our friends, not with anyone we don't know." "E-mail only our friends and only open e-mails from them." "Finish our homework when we first come home from school and before we get on the computer." "And, if our grades go down, AOL will be gone for good."

Yes, they definitely had gotten the message. They knew there were things they had to do, they knew they had to behave in a certain way, and they knew there were consequences if they didn't.

"Who's got a pen?" Angelica asked. But Michael was the first to sign. He was the oldest and, in this kind of situation, he would take the lead. One by one, the three oldest kids put their names on the bottom of the paper with the rules.

At the Office . . .

All organizations have a purpose. Nonprofit ones have certain goals. Trade associations have an important mission. Educational institutions have a mandate.

Corporations are in the business of developing, producing, and delivering valued products or services to their customers or clients.

Nonprofit companies, educational institutions, trade associations, and government organizations may charge a price or a fee for what they provide, but only for-profit organizations have the responsibility to make a profit in order to return money to their investors or shareholders.

In a nutshell, these are *commercial* enterprises. And every employee of the corporation needs to participate in making it profitable. Anyone who doesn't contribute in some form to the profitability of the enterprise quite simply shouldn't be there.

But even in nonprofit organizations of any kind, a key role of management is to make sure that each individual has a definite goal on which he or she is focused.

Productivity—and profitability—can't happen without clearly defined tasks, responsibilities, and measurable objectives. In order to center an employee's attention on what is most important for the organization, you need to identify those tasks which he or she must do during a year or other designated period of time. The employee must "sign off" on those assignments. And then you must hold that person accountable.

There are very few organizations today that don't have job descriptions. Defined roles and responsibilities are a well-established component of an effective Human Resources Department. These job descriptions are important, but, on their own, they aren't enough to get the job done. It's like saying that Michael's job description is "to be a kid, doing what a kid of his age does, plus he has to brush his teeth, do his homework, play and get along with his family and friends."

Defining roles is only the first step toward meeting today's need for increased productivity. And that's especially true when more and more companies are trying to trade some of what was fixed compensation for pay or bonuses which are awarded based on an employee's actual contribution to the company's financial success each year.

These financial incentives are very important. And defined objectives are definitely important, especially when it comes to those employees eligible for some kind of extra reward, incentive compensation, bonus, or promotion.

But what drives behavior even more directly is how those objectives are set, how they are monitored, and how they are enforced. In other words, have specific goals been established? Can they be objectively measured? Does everyone agree on them—do they amount to a deal? Are there periodic discussions appraising performance against those objectives? Finally, are there consequences if those agreed-upon goals are not met?

Keep in Mind . . .

Kids, adults, employees—we all need to know our role and what we are expected to accomplish. We need to know that the goals we've agreed to meet are important, and that we are accountable for how we perform against them. As you develop performance-based incentive systems for your staff, keep the following in mind:

❑ *Make sure everyone knows the goals of the corporation as a whole and why they are important.* Individual goals must fit within the overall goals of the company, so your staff has to understand the context in which they do certain jobs and *why* their performance counts. You cannot ask people to buy into, let alone enthusiastically take on, a task whose importance they don't grasp.

❑ *Make goal setting an active and participatory process— but make sure the goals relate to the organization's strategy.* The goals must be focused on the organization's mission and purpose. You can't leave it up to the individual employees to set the goals, but they must participate. When they do, they are even more committed. When they've been able to have input, it becomes their goal. They will often do far better than you might have expected.

❑ *Put those goals in simple, easy-to-understand language.* Don't get philosophical or use abstract words. Keep your explanations short and simple, so everyone can identify with the goals you are setting and see just how they fit in.

❑ *Translate the goals into individual actions.* Again, keep it simple. But take pains to sit down with each member of your staff to explain how he or she—individually and as part of the team—has an impact on the success of the entire enterprise.

❑ *Create a written agreement for those performance goals.* If you are going to be able to measure how well the job was done, everyone needs to see the goals in writing. Unfortunately, our memories are never perfect. Write down the points you've discussed. Read them through together. Still agreed? Are they realistic? Can they be achieved? Do they motivate? Good. Get started.

❑ *Get everyone to sign that agreement.* Get the individual employee to sign. Get the supervisor to sign. The chief executive signs, too. That way, everyone is a partner: The priorities are identified, the goals agreed upon, and performance evaluations expected. Perhaps most important, "signing off" on the agreement involves an emotional "signing on" by the employee.

❏ *Keep repeating your goals over and over.* No one gets it the first time. Don't be boring or obviously repetitious, but find different ways to remind your staff how important it is to reach these goals. Like advertising or any other communications medium, corporate goals and messages must be sent often and in a number of ways.

❏ *Reward great work.* Be supportive all along the way and fulfill your role—implicit or explicit—in the deal by rewarding great work. If you promised a reward, keep that promise.

❏ *If goals haven't been met, do something about it.* Keep in mind that it actually is insulting to hard-working staff members if you let others get away with doing less than their best work—it's not only disheartening and demoralizing, but it also sets up a double standard. This is both unfair and counterproductive. Everyone must do his part. The one who doesn't has to be called to account for it.

SEVENTEEN

The Tongue of a Different Color

No hiding from the truth

At Home . . .

The sound was unmistakable. You knew immediately it was breaking glass. It didn't even take a second to register. We hadn't seen the ball fly across the street but we saw the rear window of the Caravan shatter. The window turned into a thousand tiny, almost-square pieces that flew to the right and the left, then fell onto the driveway.

There was that deep sigh which rose from the pit of your stomach, fear about someone getting cut. But, thankfully, we could see right away that none of the five boys were hurt. And getting another window for the car wasn't as much a big deal as it, undoubtedly, would be very inconvenient.

It shouldn't have happened in the first place, but accidents do happen. Now we had to do our best to make sure that it wouldn't happen again.

Some of the children dropped their mitts, the ball and the bat. The others quickly stopped talking and looked in our direction. The five boys came over—of course, rather slowly—at least one of them feeling just a little guilty.

They knew what the questions would be. "So, how'd it happen? And who threw the ball that broke the car window?"

Those weren't angry questions. Even though the boys weren't even teenagers yet, taking responsibility was something they had to do. Learning to accept responsibility is part of growing up.

At first, no one answered.

"Let's see your tongue," Mom and Dad said, almost simultaneously.

Four out of the five were quick. Out came their tongues. They had nothing to hide. They were innocent and they knew it. They were sure that their tongues wouldn't be any color other than pink. But the guilty one—that was a different matter. He wasn't sure if his tongue would be a different color or not. And he didn't want to take the risk.

So he just stood there. He couldn't see his tongue. He stood there, rigid, his hand clamped tightly over his mouth, determined that no one would be able to catch even a faint glimpse of his tongue—which might declare to everyone by its color that he had not told the truth.

That child, even at the age of five, grasped that if he wasn't telling the truth, someone would know. Somehow, he would be found out. And he was. What he didn't know was that he gave himself away. He was found out by his own actions.

At the Office . . .

Just like children, adults, more often than not, will do something out of the ordinary when they aren't telling the truth. They will do something which they think covers up the truth. And, just like the child who immediately clasps his hand over his mouth to avoid showing his tongue, the adult will give himself away.

In the office, the first principle is obvious.

Of course, it is integrity. Your goal is to make sure that the standards of behavior in your company are very high—very high indeed. The guidelines must be clear. There is no substitute for being honest and straightforward. And your staff needs to know that nothing less will be tolerated.

The second principle is not so obvious. It is also important that your staff understands that you actually do know more than they think you do.

Once they get to thinking about that, they will instinctively recognize that you do have access to more information than they do. They will realize that you do have more sources and resources to draw on than might have occurred to them.

With that in the back of their minds, they will think twice about being anything other than straightforward. They'll shy away from corporate "games."

The work environment will be strong. And people throughout the organization will waste far less time on things which are just plain unproductive.

Keep in Mind . . .

Creating an environment where honesty and straightforward communication are mandatory can be difficult to achieve, but it is critical to a healthy organization. There are a few things you can do to help:

❏ *Be straightforward.* Don't try to fool your colleagues or subordinates, even if you may be tempted. It destroys your credibility and everyone will know. People don't like being "played." Honesty begets honesty. If it is clear to your staff that you are being straightforward with them, they will know that the best approach is to be straightforward with you.

❏ *Be visible.* There is nothing like walking around and "just stopping by" someone's office or work area to talk informally. You learn more about what's going on during this kind of informal visit than you do during a more formal meeting. And your staff *sees* that you are in touch with the organization and seeing things with your own eyes.

❏ *Learn who the informal opinion leaders are in your organization.* Talk to them often. Listen closely to what you are being told, but be sure to make your own assessment of the facts at hand.

❏ *Don't hesitate to challenge.* If you have doubts about what you're being told, challenge the conclusion and then press for the facts, letting the individual know that you will check it out for yourself.

❏ *Don't be naïve.* Unfortunately, there are some people who will cut corners, play "games," or try to get away with things they know they shouldn't be doing. Sometimes they think doing those things will get them ahead faster. Don't be naïve. And make sure your staff knows you aren't.

❏ *Don't let yourself be "played."* It takes hard work to avoid being influenced. When people tell you what's going on, be sophisticated as you listen. Be strong and confident. Make judgments for yourself.

❑ *Integrity is one of the most critical elements of leadership.* There is no substitute for being honest. There is an Italian proverb which, when loosely translated, says: *Deceit has short legs.* And it's true. You can't run from the truth.

EIGHTEEN

Surf's Up . . . Castles in the Sand

Work hard, play hard: A winning combination

At Home . . .

It was a hot August day. The front edge of the wave was white as the water churned at the curl. Tips of deep green caught in the white caps as the tide moved the late summer seaweed from the bottom of the ocean through the swirls and onto the beach. The surf rolled down the beach from left to right as the Atlantic pounded the sand on its way to nowhere.

Weekends that summer were filled with long days by the ocean in the sunshine. The blue of James and

Michael's eyes almost jumped out at you, set off by their tans and wavy bright blond hair.

In the morning, as the rest of us got our things together for the walk to the beach, the two older boys took their surfboards off the racks in the garage and started down the street toward the boardwalk. Each of those surfboards was at least two feet longer than either of the boys. And even though the fiberglass was so light you could have lifted it with one finger, Michael and James struggled every day to tuck the board under an arm, balance its length, front and back, and carry it to the water's edge.

Once there, they strapped the Velcro at the end of the lanyard around their left ankles and bravely walked into the water, dragging their feet as they went. If all you saw was the trail in the sand, you would have guessed that a ball and chain had left the image, not two kids off for another early morning attempt at surfing.

The waves were usually damped down by the heat at midday, only to build up again as the sun slid lower on the horizon and eventually fell off the edge of the earth.

When the surfing got to be too much, the boys would sit on top of their boards, their feet hanging down into the water, and watch the more experienced surfers as they caught the waves and stood up. When the boys had truly had enough, they would lie down on the board with a sigh and paddle toward shore.

As they neared the shore and the board slid onto the sand, their interests veered quickly toward the sodas, the sandwiches, and the cookies that had waited in the cooler all morning.

Almost as quickly, thoughts turned to sandcastles and the kids ran off to the water's edge again. The tide was low and the beach was deep. And this time it took even more steps to cross the damp sand and reach the water.

The castle walls were built thick to hold back the onrushing tide. The parapets on top were neatly cut out of damp sand, and there was a road through the hillside for the plastic cars and trucks that came to the beach with us every day. The sandcastle grew. It got taller. Firmer. When some of the sand started to dry, the boys wet it down with sea water so it wouldn't crumble and fall. Deep inside the castle, the two littlest kids could stand, although the water was up to their ankles. According to the old fisherman, who always came to that same spot each day to surf cast and look for the perfect striped bass, water came up through the center of the earth from China.

No, of course they didn't really believe him. Both Michael and James were far too old and experienced for that. But it was sort of fun to imagine what it would be like to see someone emerge from the sand like Bluebeard. You see, they knew the story about that notorious pirate who was buried up to his neck on the beach so that the oncoming water would slowly cover his head and torture him as the tide moved higher and higher.

Right, there was no Bluebeard. But the tide did slowly move up the beach. And, as it did, the sandcastle crumbled, the foundation eroding first and then the walls tumbling down.

It was a terrific summer for the whole family. But finally the excitement of all the surfing, the sandcastles, the Boogie boards, and riding the waves also began to erode, and the kids began to get restless. The summer was waning—the sun was lower on the horizon—and so were its pleasures. The sun was also setting earlier and earlier each day. You started needing a jacket or a sweatshirt as you sat on the beach to watch the sun go down.

By late August, not only Michael and James, but the younger kids too were getting more and more irritable. Their early-summer fantasies had worn thin. The wonder of digging for sand crabs in June had become just another "same old thing" to do. And if we couldn't conjure up something new to occupy their every moment, they were quick to complain that they were bored.

It was always the same with the kids as summer drew to a close. The body, the mind, the spirit had run free for almost three months. Now their innards knew it was time to return to school. It was time to get some order, some discipline, and some goals back in their lives. And *we* knew that they would be ready to start school in September with the kind of energy and curiosity that we always hoped they'd bring to it.

At the Office . . .

One of the most difficult issues to deal with in managing people is how to find the right balance between hard work and time off.

In today's very competitive marketplace, productivity is of enormous consequence. And, quite frankly, at times the temptation is great to push for more work at the expense of time off. In fact, it's far too common for the message to be conveyed, whether directly or indirectly, that it would be preferable for people to defer vacations in the interest of getting more work done.

There is no question: Doing exactly that is sometimes essential in order to meet a deadline or to have certain key people—people with an irreplaceable talent—available to complete a crucial assignment.

But you can't send that message too often.

There's a time for work and there is a time for play. People seem to need some external force to help provide order and purpose in their lives. Getting up and going to work and tackling problems in a systematic but thoughtful manner provide that order for many people.

And even though people must have the chance to go on vacation—do interesting, stimulating, and *different* things during their time off—they also need to come back to work. They need the order. They need the discipline. They need the structure.

But while they are away, they need to have every chance to *be* away.

Given a thorough getaway, people will be ready to come back to work. Just like kids who, as the summer wanes, become increasingly bored and restless, there is a time to return to the welcome order of daily life.

Keep in Mind . . .

Believe it or not, one of your jobs as a leader is to help people keep balance in their lives. That means you need to look to your own patterns and think about what kind of effect your decisions and your actions have on your staff. Consider the following:

❏ *Don't play the martyr.* Take vacations yourself. You deserve it. You'll be better for it. And you will set the right example.

❏ *Actively encourage your staff to take vacations.* The impulse—especially by those who are very ambitious and career driven—is to forgo vacations for the sake of work. Don't let that happen. Encourage staff members to take the regular vacations they're entitled to. If necessary, *urge* them to get away for a while. You can't force them to take a vacation, of course, but make sure you let them know you think they should.

❑ *As soon as employees return from vacation, get them involved, immediately, in some difficult task or project.* They are ready to be re-engaged. In fact, they are looking to get going on something, even if they don't realize it. Moreover, energized, they will bring new ideas and, perhaps most important, enthusiasm to whatever challenge you place before them on their return.

❑ *Keep your own life in balance.* The truth is, your company can go on and be successful without you, so don't be foolish. Yes, you can be replaced. And the castle you build today can collapse tomorrow. So don't lose the balance in your own life. Rather, use it to your advantage. Get out of the office. Go on a vacation or, at least, get away for a few days. You'll come back refreshed, with a surge of new energy. And probably a sensational idea or two. Maybe even half a dozen.

NINETEEN

When to Dive in the Deep End

Going where you've never been before

At Home . . .

He really was pretty good in the shallow end. Then again, it was only three feet deep and Michael was by now taller than that. After all, he was six years old and at the stage when he was beginning to develop the kind of self-confidence which gave him strength in unfamiliar situations, maybe even when they were a little scary.

And he'd been swimming around in the shallow end of the pool ever since he could remember. By now, he knew that, if he stood on his toes, he could actually walk along the bottom of the swimming pool with the water reaching only to his chin. That gave him a degree of comfort. It also made him a little braver.

With that extra bit of confidence, he had decided it was time to try something new. He'd started to swim underwater. He would take a deep breath, kick off from one side, and do his best to make it to the other side without having to come up for air. But every time so far, he'd had to give up part way across.

You could see that he really preferred it when no one was watching. Maybe that took at least the external pressure off. With no one to comment or offer advice, he'd just have himself to do battle with.

Anyway, he kept trying. He'd obviously thought it through. Yet, if you brought up the subject, he always shied away. He never confided his strategy or how he thought he was doing. But every day that summer, he would go to the pool and, at first, sit next to the lifeguard for a little while. Sometimes he would ask Darryn to tell him some of the tricks he'd learned about surfing—he never tired of hearing the answers. Other times, he was curious to find out if Darryn ever got scared when all those red jellyfish started coming around in August. You could see the two of them sitting over there, talking— intent in a world of their own. In fact, Michael wouldn't have liked it if he knew anyone could hear them. Those conversations were supposed to be just between the two of them.

When he felt ready, he would get in the pool and start swimming around. Then, suddenly—a couple of deep breaths the only clue—he would duck his head under the water and head towards the other side. Watching from across the pool as he headed toward you, you could see that his eyes were wide open. It fascinated us that Michael's arms seemed to move faster than his legs. It was almost as if he were pulling himself across the pool.

One afternoon, as we watched, we sensed that today would be the day. Every stroke said nothing would stop Michael from making it across this time.

He did . . . of course. One breath and he crossed the pool underwater. When he reached the other side, he jumped up and down and yelled out, "I did it!" Three simple words. But, put together like that, they meant the world to this young boy.

So, what was next? To our surprise, he told us. Maybe he'd really had it in mind for weeks. He'd been watching the summer Olympics and, perhaps even more important, he'd seen other kids dive into the pool and race down its length toward the shallow end. Now it was his turn to dive.

Unlike swimming underwater, this he did want to talk about. "Dad," he asked, "how do I make sure I don't hit the bottom? How do I keep from belly flopping?"

"You need to keep your head down and your ears tucked between your arms. Then you can do it."

But words weren't enough. "Dad, show me," he said.

Together, we knelt by the edge of the pool. He remembered what Dad had told him and bent his head down. Dad put his arms against his ears and offered to give him a gentle push. But he didn't want that.

He looked at Dad wordlessly—not wanting to hurt any feelings—but his face said that he wanted to do it by himself. Getting it right, on his own, would prove to him that, if it was possible for others, it was possible for him.

Dad stood up and stepped back.

Michael knelt down again. He positioned himself correctly. You could hear him counting quietly to himself, "One . . . two . . . three . . . go." He leaned over and in he went. A "perfect ten" at the Olympics could not have been high enough to reflect the triumph of that first dive. Michael had made a decision to go where he had never been before. And he had gone there. By himself.

His smile said it all.

At the Office . . .

Doing what you might have thought impossible. Taking chances. Challenging yourself to try something different—even with a risk attached. These are the moments that create the opportunity for real success.

Children sense these moments strongly. Then, like adults, they tackle them, each in his or her very own way.

Like theirs, our success will be determined by how each of us deals with the many challenges we face.

In our organizations, we face difficult decisions and choices on a daily basis. Some of them have an impact on our staff. Some on our customers. And others on those many people with whom we have business relationships and who can help us be successful, if they so choose.

Some of those decisions may seem of monumental consequence. A few of them turn out to be just that. Others end up being—merely—important. Some seem trivial. Of these, a few may turn out to be far from trivial. But even small decisions matter. And they add up. Indeed, all our decisions are cumulative.

We are judged by the courage with which we make those decisions, large and small. That's only fair. We are also judged by the actions we take after we've made one choice or another—and that, too, is fair.

But, even more important than being fair, it's a reality of life: *Our decisions stand for us.*

There are some extraordinary moments when we go where we have never been before. And, regardless of whether we are in a swimming pool or in a corner office, those journeys are not only an essential part of how the world sees us, but they're also an essential element in how we see ourselves.

Keep in Mind . . .
The first ingredient of success is being ready to try. Being
ready and willing to accept a challenge. To go for it. That
takes courage. Think about the following:

❏ *Take a chance.* Whether it's in your personal career
choices or your business decisions, don't be afraid to
take a chance. Success goes to those who are willing
to do something new—or do something in a new
way. The old Russian proverb—*He who doesn't risk,
doesn't win*—is an admonition to consider. Often, it
is through taking a chance that people discover—in
themselves, in their field, in the world—something
they never knew existed. Even if it doesn't turn out
well, it could be worthwhile, simply because you
learned something important which you would
never have learned had you not made that decision.

❏ *Listen to other viewpoints.* Present the facts of a problem to those whose intellect and experience you
trust. Ask the advice of specialists. But don't ever lose
sight of your own perspective, because ultimately
that's what you have to rely on.

❏ *Get enough information . . . but not too much.* Don't
let yourself, as they say, succumb to "paralysis by
analysis."

❏ *Don't over-think things.* When you know what should
be done, get it done. Don't squander time or effort
constructing a rationale for your decision. You don't

have to make every decision acceptable to everyone else. Almost always, the results will confirm your judgment.

❑ *Trust your gut.* You know instinctively what is right. Don't go against what your gut tells you. Listen to your instincts and go in the direction they lead.

❑ *Don't put off until this afternoon the decision you can make this morning.* Make choices sooner rather than later. Few businesspeople regret having moved fast to make a decision. But many businesspeople regret having waited too long to do what they intuitively knew immediately was the right thing. Don't do things hastily. Take the time you need. But don't delay.

❑ *Don't ever forget—it's not only what you do, but how you do it.* If you want support for your decision, think through how it will be accepted—or it might be rejected by others. Anticipate how others will see your action. Pave the way for it. Don't shy away from what you know is right. But do it well. Give it your best shot.

❑ *Go ahead and make the decision.* It would be nice to lead by consensus, but sometimes it just isn't practical—or even possible. So when it is your decision to make, get on with it.

❑ *It takes courage to be the boss.* But that's one of the reasons why you *are* the boss.

TWENTY

When Things Get Tough

Coming to grips with the unexpected

At Home ...

No one has a crystal ball. It was the middle of June and the little bit of water still left on the street after the last night's rain was slowly disappearing with the heat of the rising sun. As usual, you could count on the yellow school bus to come down the road, the driver to flash the red lights, pull to a stop, then push the long lever and open the door on time.

Today, James turned ten. It was a big deal. As we say in our family, *"Double digits at last."* His birthday gifts on the kitchen table that morning had heightened the morning's excitement. And, of course, this was all against a backdrop where the kids were already eager for school to come to a close and summer to begin.

Mom—for reasons which can really only be understood as *"a mother's instinct"*—didn't somehow feel right about James as she watched him lift the backpack over his shoulder and walk more slowly than usual toward the bus stop. At first, she didn't pay too much attention to her concerns. Yes, he'd had a cold, strep throat in fact. But that wasn't uncommon in a home with six kids. Maybe, she thought, it simply was one of those more-than-hectic mornings. But…she couldn't help but linger longer, standing on the top step of the stoop and watching him until he rounded the corner.

Then, just when she should have turned and headed back into the house, she knew that he shouldn't go to school that day. Going through a rush of thoughts and emotions, she tried to pull all of the details together: strep for sure, but beyond that he'd sometimes been feeling weak, had lost weight, drank more than usual, and even once felt dizzy. We even all sort of joked about the weight loss—you know, *a growing boy, getting taller and thinning out; an extra hot fudge sundae should do the trick to put some meat on those bones.*

Now, though, Mom wasn't about to let him go to school. She called his name out loud, hoping that the bus hadn't already come. When she saw James emerge from the crowd of kids waiting for the bus, she knew he wasn't well enough to go to school. It was the way he was dragging his backpack now and how he hung his head. Not like James. Mom called for him to come back home. Her first thought was that James might need a stronger prescription for his strep throat. Or, maybe it was mono.

Within the hour, James was at the doctor. All Mom could hear was our family pediatrician, Dr. Jonisch, asking, "Do you have any history of diabetes in your family?" His blood sugar had just been tested at 775.

"No," she answered, "at least not that we know."

When they got to the hospital and James was tested again, his blood sugar was still very high. His Hemoglobin A_{1c}—the more critical, long-term test to determine how much sugar remains in the blood for extended periods of time—was 16.6. All of Mom's worries had pointed to the classic symptoms of the onset of juvenile diabetes, Type 1—or insulin dependent diabetes. The test had just confirmed it

At the hospital, on a bed in one of the corners of the emergency room, James was being given intravenous fluids because he was dehydrated. Also, he was being given insulin to bring his blood sugar level down. His pancreas, we were told, was not producing nearly enough insulin on its own.

None of us ever expected any of this. We were to learn a lot that day. All of it vital. And much of it directed not only at James, but also at Mom and Dad.

The emergency room attending physician and the

nurses were helpful and reassuring. But when the endocrinologist, Dr. Cecilia Cervantes, arrived we really knew we were in good hands. She took control quickly and explained as much as she could with absolute clarity.

Type 1 diabetes happens most often in children. It is what is known as an autoimmune disease. This means that the body has developed antibodies that are destroying one's own cells. In James's case, those antibodies were destroying the insulin-producing islet cells of his pancreas. Then, because he couldn't produce enough insulin, James's body was not able to properly convert sugar to energy. Instead, the sugar level was building up in his blood and the only recourse his body had was to try to get rid of the sugar through his kidneys. When that happened, James started to become weak. He was also always very thirsty and began to lose weight.

The simple fact is that without insulin body tissue cannot absorb sugar. And, over time, if the blood has too much sugar, the body can develop very serious acute and long-term complications. In a nutshell, that was happening to James.

Sometimes, the onset of diabetes is preceded by some sort of "shock" to the body. Yes, James had strep throat when he was diagnosed. And, he had broken his arm—in two places, actually—in March while doing jumps off a ramp on his Rollerblades. Maybe that contributed. Maybe not.

But none of that really mattered. In fact, the task at

hand was to learn how to deal with it in order to keep the blood sugar under control. Dr. Cervantes said that James would be in the hospital for about a week. Of course, we didn't understand why. And it was her answer that really shocked us. "The three of you will be in the hospital for a week, not so much for him," she said, "but for you!"

A week in the hospital. We knew how he felt. It was his birthday. That very week was his graduation from grammar school, and the class, so proud of their accomplishments, had practiced for a month. It was the week of his very first dance with the other fifth graders. We couldn't help but ask ourselves, *Why?* And *Why this week for James?* So many memories that were to have gone in the shoebox he kept under his bed—now gone.

But the nurses in the hospital were great at helping James keep things in perspective. They decorated the walls around his bed with posters and Happy Birthday wishes. Just no cake and candy . . . at least not yet.

All three of us were the ones who had to learn. We had to know what was going on. We had to learn what would need to be done. And we would have to understand our role in helping James handle this.

So, for almost seven days, Mom and Dad took turns spending the night on a cot by James. During the day, the three of us listened together to nutritionists and practiced: taking blood sugar levels, measuring insulin, filling syringes, and giving shots. We did it to ourselves to feel what it was really like. We did it to each other to make sure. We did it with James. And, most important, James learned to do it for himself.

The three of us learned how to count carbohydrates—commonly known by diabetics and their families as "carb counting"—surprisingly, one of the most difficult tasks in the attempt to measure insulin treatments with some accuracy.

James was the best student of all. He was quick at math, understood the formulas for deciding on how much insulin to measure, and how to fill the syringe.

James's sister Vera, an emergency room nurse, and Sirish, the third-year general surgery resident doctor whom she would marry almost exactly two years later, immediately came from their jobs in Manhattan to be at the hospital within an hour of James being admitted. Their compassion and experience helped guide us as we came to grips with the disease and how it would affect our lives.

By the end of the week, we pretty much had it together. At least enough, everyone agreed, to let us leave the hospital. But, when we all checked out, it wasn't without a healthy dose of trepidation.

It really was James who, when he left that day, was the best adjusted. He had come to grips with what he faced and was ready to deal with it.

The next few days fast became a blur. We made lists, drew charts detailing *what happens if,* put medical supplies in special places, made notes for each other, drew up schedules of what to eat and when, mounted bulletin boards in the kitchen with instructions and emergency numbers. And we were on the phone at least twice a day with Dr. Cervantes to hear her voice, get her opinion, and feel her comfort.

But, most of all, there was James. And, as each day went by and his blood sugar levels remained within the range of 80 to 140, we knew he was getting better. He felt stronger and stronger. He played baseball that summer in Little League. He went to camp. He played roller hockey on the street again. And, when school started again in September, he was doing great. He'd even put back some of the weight he'd lost.

Still, though, we knew we had to remain focused. We had no choice but to concentrate on identifying what we had to do and simply going about doing it. The regimen helped. There were people to involve—the school, family, friends—and we learned about an increasingly larger group of people who were in similar situations. Their insights were invaluable.

By October, James's Hemoglobin A_{1c} was 6.4! This was a milestone. It had descended below the crucial threshold of 7 and was where it should be. It also was a good indication that his diabetes could be managed. And that James was in control of his diabetes and not the other way around.

Throughout the first year, our goal was to better understand the situation and deal with it. There were tough times when it seemed as if it was almost too diffi-cult to control the blood sugar levels. But we had no choice but to keep at it. James's immediate health was our primary concern, and everything we did was directed toward that goal.

When James became even the slightest bit interested in how an insulin pump could make his daily routine eas-ier and more flexible—allowing him to sleep later, eat when he wanted, try new foods, have that occasional hot fudge sundae, or a few candies on Halloween—we looked into it.

James now wears an insulin pump. This is an incred-ible machine he keeps in his pocket around the clock. It's about the size of a beeper. It delivers insulin on a regular basis throughout each day. It can be programmed to deliver additional insulin doses at meals, snacks, and when the blood sugar level might be high. He knows the ins and outs of the pump and how to make it work by pressing the buttons even without looking—with such a great attitude, it has become second nature to him.

As the months went on, we took what we had learned and focused our energies in a slightly different direction. Our perspective changed somewhat. We were no less focused on James's health but now we could put our minds to learning more about the disease and the potential for finding a cure. The energies that at the out-set we directed toward what some might call "survival," we now directed toward the future.

That perspective led to our involvement with the Juvenile Diabetes Research Foundation and its enormously valuable contributions to scientific research.

This has become the overarching emotion for James, his brothers and sisters, and Mom and Dad. We tell everyone, *"Together we can find a cure for diabetes and we will do it within our lifetime."*

At the Office . . .

Dealing with adversity, especially the unexpected kind, is a fact of life. And it applies equally in business as it does in the family.

In fact, the business environment that has launched this century has, unquestionably, been one of the most difficult in years. Around the world, pressures caused by depressed economies, turmoil in the financial markets, and political tensions in many countries have come together to create what many would have earlier thought was unexpected.

On the one hand, the truth is that no one can predict the future. No one in business can say for sure what will happen—and no one has. And no one in business can look back and legitimately say that they knew what would happen. Clearly, no one could claim to have known or anticipated the confluence of events that characterize these times.

On the other hand, though, we do need to be disciplined and strategic enough in our planning to try and anticipate the unexpected. We can't anticipate everything, but looking at barriers, potential problems, and worst-case scenarios is an important component of any strategic business plan.

Yet, even the best planning cannot anticipate everything. There will always be *the unexpected*. It is a fact of life.

As Mom and Dad, neither of us could have anticipated diabetes. We'd never even talked about it. It wasn't part of our family histories. There was no reason to have thought much about it, except when the disease affected close friends and others we knew.

But this was tough for us. And it was unexpected. Like so many difficult moments, they come when you least expect them, and you are least prepared.

Unfortunately, when confronted with the unexpected, too often the first reaction as a parent or a manager can be shock, and that can be soon followed by fear or denial. In those situations, the quick response too often takes one of these forms: *No way! Not me! Not us! Not at our company. I don't believe it. That can't be true. It's never happened before this way. We're too smart for that. I'm sure we thought of everything.*

Those are natural reactions. We all have to confess that we feel that way sometimes. But those reactions don't do us any good. Whether in our personal lives—our family lives—or our businesses, that way of thinking doesn't enable us to get beyond the problem and try to solve it. More often than not, it simply makes things worse.

Keep in Mind . . .

When we come face-to-face with the unexpected—and things get tough—there are some points to remember:

❑ *First, get your act together.* Quickly get beyond the shock. Get beyond the emotional reaction. Take a deep breath. Keep calm. Purposeful action is constructive. Overreaction—or even action simply for action's sake—can be destructive.

❑ *Second, don't go into denial. Just get on with it.* Don't underestimate the severity of the problem. It could happen to you. You are the leader and have to be strong. Accept what is real. Recognize the problem for what it is and deal with it.

❑ *Third, take the situation apart.* Break it into bite-sized pieces so that you can tackle it one part at a time. Too much will be overwhelming. Take it one stage at a time.

❑ *Fourth, focus on survival and get things stabilized.* Work to create an environment where people can go about doing their tasks so that the core of what needs to be done does get done. Keep the company doing what the company does best. Keep people focused. The core business must continue to function and function well, even when the going is tough.

❏ *Fifth, learn the new things you now must know.* Get on with it. Learn. Start using your new skills to lead the business into new areas and create the opportunity for eventual success. And make sure the others are learning new skills and using those tools well.

❏ *Sixth, set your sights far enough to create a long-term goal in spite of the buffeting of the short-term problem.* Look out ahead. That's your job as the leader, the manager, the boss, even the chief executive. That long-term view is like a beacon to a ship or an airplane. It unites people and keeps them on track even when they might otherwise have doubts.

❏ *And seventh, create a vision for the future and do it with emotion.* Be realistic but paint a positive picture with strategy, words, and ideas. It's your job as the leader to give people hope. You set the emotional tone that carries people through difficult times and beyond.

Afterword

I t's all about perspective.

When we think about the home and about the workplace, we see parallels. To us, the link is as natural as *peanut butter and jelly*. We came to that view after watching what went on with our own children at home and then, over time, noticing similarities at work. This perspective is at the heart of our book.

Now, as we continue to think about behavior at work, it is increasingly clear to us that, beyond the Internet, management continues to be one of the great frontiers in business. It's where new insights into people, behavior and motivations give us the opportunity to create organizations that are even more successful and strong.

That being the case, it seems to us that soon more and more of the articles and books on business will focus on the idea that successful corporate leaders of the coming decade will have to be "people persons."

If these leaders *are* "people persons," they're going to begin their stewardship by tackling some critical questions. *How should we lead our employees? How do they feel about the organization, the environment in which they work, and the leadership? What motivates them to excel? How can we develop the most productive behavior? What must employees do to deliver on the business strategy and to produce the kind of financial results that are worthy of a first-class company? And, most importantly, how does leadership make that happen?*

Clearly, the home can't provide answers to all those questions. And the fact is that no one—no matter how experienced—has all the answers. Even so, tomorrow's leaders may well find some guidance here because parenting is one of the toughest jobs on earth. It just may be *the* toughest job.

Certainly, parenting heads the list of leadership positions that call for a "people person." We both work hard at being that. And so we'd like to share these ten closing thoughts that have helped us—with our family and with business:

❏ Be a leader first—and a manager second.

❏ Be attentive—watch, listen, observe, think about what is going on—remembering always that you and everyone around you are only human.

❑ Communicate, communicate, and communicate more.

❑ Create a fabric of strong values—and live them yourself every day.

❑ Don't ask anyone to do anything you wouldn't do yourself.

❑ Build self-esteem in others.

❑ Create a team—work with and through others: Delegate and give them the skills and tools to do their job.

❑ Focus your energy on those things that are really important.

❑ Have confidence in yourself.

❑ You're on center stage—everyone is watching.

Index

The Komisarjevsky family. From left to right: Nicholas, Vera, Matthew, Katrina, Dad, Mom, Michael (on top of slide), James, Ted, Angelica, and Stephen.

About the Authors

Chris and Reina Komisarjevsky have a family filled with children. When everyone is together, there's lots of activity, excitement, caring—and, naturally, some disagreements.

Reina is a full-time Mom who always wished she would have at least six children. She grew up the second youngest in a family of five children in Queens, New

York. She remembers a neighborhood where the street was the playground for throwing a softball. Her father, a chef born in Switzerland, taught her the art of baking and she inherited his passion for getting it just right. And she will never forget the image of her mother, leaning out of the second story window of their two-family house, watching closely and anxiously waiting for her girls to come home, walking down the street.

Chris is a full-time Dad and the president and chief executive officer of Burson-Marsteller. He grew up in a family of six children, two families brought together in a second marriage after the mother of two and the father of three passed away—then a sixth was born of that new marriage. His mother was one of the pioneers of modern dance and, with a special ability to sense what was going on in a child's mind, she opened her own dance school. Chris' early memories are shaped by the time he spent playing among costumes when his own father directed theater in New York City. And he looks back with great fondness on the years when his stepfather introduced him to tennis, hockey, and writing.

After graduating from college and then spending five years in the U.S. Army—reaching the rank of Captain and serving as a helicopter pilot in Vietnam—Chris went to graduate school, on to work in New York and then to Europe. Now working from the Burson-Marsteller world-wide headquarters in New York City, he has responsibility for the business with two thousand professionals across the globe. As a public relations professional, he has counseled chief executives, senior management, and communications professionals from private and public companies in a wide range of industries whose operations are both in the United States and throughout the world. He has authored articles on communications and business and lectured at graduate schools. Chris has a bachelor's degree in political science and a master's degree in business. He is a 1996 recipient of the Ellis Island Medal of Honor, serves on the boards of a number of nonprofit organizations and as a trustee of a mutual fund company.

Chris and Reina wrote this book together—simply because they are partners, they learned from each other and from each of the children, and one could never have done it alone.